God—Moses—Me

God—Moses—Me

Conversations with God

Stephen Schey

ARPress
ILLUMINATING IDEAS
EMPOWERING VOICES

ARPress
45 Dan Road Suite 5
Canton MA 02021

Hotline: 1(888) 821-0229
Fax: 1(508) 545-7580

Ordering Information:

Quantity sales. Special discounts are available on quantity purchases by corporations, associations, and others. For details, contact the publisher at the address above.

All Scripture quotations, unless otherwise indicated, are taken from the Holy Bible, New International Version®, NIV®. Copyright ©1973, 1978, 1984, 2011 by Biblica, Inc.™ Used by permission of Zondervan. All rights reserved worldwide. www.zondervan.com The "NIV" and "New International Version" are trademarks registered in the United States Patent and Trademark Office by Biblica, Inc.™

Printed in the United States of America.

ISBN-13:	Softcover	979-8-89356-052-7
	eBook	979-8-89356-053-4
	Hardcover	979-8-89356-054-1

Library of Congress Control Number: 2024903372

DEDICATION

I am so grateful for the support and encouragement of my wife, Ellen, who urged me to get started writing after taking a long time just thinking and talking about it. I also want to thank my brother-in-law Drew Procak who is truly a brother and friend for his encouragement but more his enthusiasm, drive and valuable insights as he reviewed drafts. I also want to thank God for the many persons who over the centuries carefully and painstakingly copied text so that we could hold God's Word in our hands.

CONTENTS

FOREWORD

Growing up, my father seemed like a giant to me when it came to faith. I remember very clearly going in to say good night to him on so many nights, and there, he would be, "Bible open," with the look on his face of someone absorbed in some important truth.

I met my father when I was four years old and believed with all my heart that God brought him to my mother and me for a very specific purpose—one that has a great deal to do with shaping our faith in God. It was no small miracle that when he met us, having not much experience with kids at that time, he took to me right away like an experienced daddy. I have often wondered with some sense of awe at the way that God provided Steve to me and believe it had made all the difference in how my life played out.

My childhood prior to that was difficult and left its share of scars. Yet Steve became my father in every sense of the word providing an example of who God is and how God loves me. Maybe in part as a result of some of those early wounds, I have had a life of ups and downs with God, often running away and giving my heart to the wrong things in this world. But I had always come back time and time again to a gracious and loving God—a god that my dad longed to make come alive in that way for you within the pages of this book. It's funny how as an adult, you see your parents differently, more as "real people" and not just parents who raised you. My dad is still a pretty cool guy, but I know he has his own struggles.

I have watched and listened as my dad's faith has continued to mature and deepen over the last twenty years. We've had some amazing discussions and some disagreements as well when talking about God, Jesus, and the Bible.

I see shades of some of those covered here in this book, and in fact, there are multiple places where these topics are very personal for me such as divorce. Many of these conversations that Moses has with God bring to life the fact that much of the truth of God's Word can be challenging to us.

There have been many times in my life when I have had a hard struggle with what God has to say to me in the Bible and known I can't possibly measure up.

However, I am also encouraged that we see the thread of God's compassionate character from the Old Testament to the New within these pages. I have come to know that what God wants from me more than anything is relationship and for me to follow Him with my whole life and whole heart.

While my father is not perfect, he and my mother have taught me so much about God as a loving parent. And while I know God calls me to something better than what the world tells is me okay, at the end of the day, He loves me like a Father. Just as my parents have loved me through some pretty big failures in my life, so does God love me perfectly, even in my imperfectness. Because the Lord is compassionate and gracious, slow to anger, abounding in love. He will not always accuse, nor will he harbor his anger forever; He does not treat us as our sins deserve or repays us according to our iniquities. For as high as the heavens are above the earth, so great is His love for those who fear Him; as far as the east is from the west, so far has He removed our transgressions from us. I pray that you will come to see and know God's character in these pages so that you can learn to hear His voice clearly in your own discussions with Him.

—Shelly Schey
(Psalm 103:8–12)

PREFACE

God was about to do a new thing. Before Moses, He had revealed himself to individuals and developed relationships with them. He was known as the God of Abraham, the God of Isaac, and the God of Jacob. He was now going to be the God of the Israelites. Moses was His choice to lead this transition.

As one of the pillars of the Jewish and Christian faiths, Moses holds a unique position. The Lord would speak to Moses face to face, as one speaks to a friend.[1] Often we like to think of these pillars in the faith as larger than life. But as we look closer into the life of Moses, we find a man like so many others, who has his own personality, strengths, and weaknesses but who when called, empowered, and supported by God, accomplishes great things.

During the forty years of wandering in the wilderness, Moses spoke regularly with God. The Bible records the covenants, laws, and requirements God directed for his chosen people but little is recorded of the "friendly" conversation. What might Moses have discussed with God in this manner?

One might suppose that the topics of discussion then might be similar to those we have today with our friends concerning our relationship with God and His relationship with His creation. Topics of this nature, of course, are pure speculation, but based upon the recorded life experiences of Moses; we might propose questions that would have been important to him and also to us.

In the Bible's recorded conversations, God does answer the questions that Moses poses and it is therefore likely that He would also respond to other questions Moses may have had. Clearly, God's answers to these supposed questions are not recorded so how might God reply? I struggled with my ineptitude in attempting to respond for God but we do know that God is the same from the beginning of creation to today. Although Moses did not have access to the entire Word of God in the Bible, we know that all scripture is God-breathed and is useful for teaching rebuking, correcting and training in righteousness.[2] Therefore, scripture informs us of God's desires and guidance for all aspects of our lives and it can be searched for replies to questions. I claim no new revelation from God in this book but rather take from the revelation that exists in His holy Word. So then, I attempt to ask questions that would be relevant to Moses's day, approximately 1,500 years before the birth of Christ but God's response can use the full text of the Bible although Moses would have been unaware of any events that occurred after his life.

To speculate on what may have been the topics of conversation, we must seriously review the man and his circumstances. Like all of us, Moses was not born with a mature understanding and faith in the Almighty. This faith and trusting relationship grew through his life experiences. There are three distinct forty-year intervals in Moses's perspective. The first forty years are away from God, the second are searching for meaning and the last forty are growth and maturity in faith. For many of us, this is a familiar pattern. The questions we encounter in our personal journey may also have been questions for Moses. I'll attempt to arrange questions in relation to this maturing.

The first two chapters will set the stage to introduce Moses and his times. The next three chapters relate to his growth in relationship with God. The final chapter provides some final thoughts about the man, his message, and relevance for today.

My style here is conversational as it would be expected in a friendly conversation. Those who know me may, in fact, recognize my personal conversational tone. This is as I have experienced my quiet times of meditation and reflection.

God's conversational style with others may be different because God knows each of us so well, and He knows how to communicate with each of us.

Although Moses is vitally important in the second through fifth books in the Bible (as well as the author of the first) and is often mentioned and cited elsewhere, very little is really know of him outside the biblical account. I found three sources especially helpful in gaining additional perspective on the man Moses.

John J. Davis. *Moses and the Gods of Egypt, Studies in Exodus*,
Winona Lake, Indiana: BMH Books, 1986

Jonathan Kirsch. *Moses, A Life, New York:* Ballentine
Books, 1998

Charles R. Swindoll. *Moses, A Man of Selfless Dedication,*
Nashville, Tennessee: Thomas Nelson publisher,
1999

All agree that little evidence of the man or his times exist in the secular record. Davis and Swindoll approach the examination of Moses from a "pious" biblical scholar viewpoint in that they both believe in the Bible as the Word of God. Kirsch approaches the topic as a secular biblical scholar. Kirsch presents information on Moses as presented from folklore and rabbinical traditions as well as the biblical accounts. While information from sources other than the Bible may be interesting, I rely primarily on the biblical account to attempt to understand Moses.

Because there is little archeological evidence for Moses and the plight of the Israelites in Egypt, there is controversy over placing the biblical events in the historical record. Because this controversy is outside my focus, I will simply accept the placement presented by Davis.

There is also disagreement concerning the authorship of the first five books of the Bible although most pious scholars attribute the authorship to Moses. I'll assume the same.

I attempt to present these topics as a dialog between God and Moses as friends speak to each other. I use normal text for Moses and red text as quoted from the Bible with references provided with endnotes. My own interjections of comments by God are shown in blue text. The New International Version (NIV) is used throughout unless otherwise noted.

I encourage the reader to study the first five books of the Bible to explore with me the man and his conversations with God. Certainly, that proposed herein is not exhaustive.

INTRODUCTION

Imagine having a casual two-way *direct* conversation with God! Imagine being in a position to be able to ask God any question and have Him provide an answer. We all really do have that opportunity through prayer and Scripture and it can be a reality for each of us. But the relationship for Moses was unique. Moses met regularly directly with God to hold friendly conversations. The Bible says that when Moses met with God his face was radiant because he had spoken with the Lord.[1] It was so radiant that it scared people and Moses had to put a veil on until the radiance dimmed.

Moses, then, is a very unique individual. Who was this person who had such an unusual upbringing, was exiled, was personally called by God into service at the age of eighty, stood up to the king of Egypt, and led the new nation of Israel through the desert for another forty years to the edge of entering the land promised by God? How did he become one of the most important figures in Judaism and Christianity? Certainly, God gave him the instructions for the Israelite's life and relationships with Him and each other that are recorded in the Bible, but what of personal conversations?

No known document other than the Bible provides a historical record of the person Moses. The Jewish religion contains rabbinical traditions and interpretations based upon the accounts recorded in the first five books of the Bible (the Pentateuch) but no secular records or accounts of the activities of the Israelites recorded in the books of Exodus, Leviticus, Numbers, and Deuteronomy are directly available. Some secular biblical scholars suggest that an individual Moses may not have existed. Such discussions are left to others and here we rely on the recorded events and the many references in the Old and New Testaments to the person Moses as sufficient proof of his personhood.

At times, God directed Moses to write this on a scroll as something to be remembered.[2] While some may dispute the authorship of the Pentateuch, Moses is so identified in the Bible and is the accepted author in this document.

As the author of the Pentateuch, much is revealed about this person. Insight into the person of Moses is gained through the discussion of his unique upbringing, early development, intimate spiritual development, and the historical placement of his mission. All of these influences are important in considering what discussions he may have had personally with God. I have posed some possibilities here and these are by no means limiting to what a man of Moses's stature could have raised. Perhaps, this may lead the reader to his/her own questions and to seek God's reply in the Bible.

FIRST FORTY YEARS
Exodus 1:1 - 2:15 (NIV)

Historical Context

We are first introduced to Moses at his birth in Egypt as recorded in Exodus chapter 2. He and the other Israelites were descended from Jacob (also named Israel), the son of Isaac, the son of Abraham. The book of Genesis records how Israel and his extended family moved from the land of Canaan to Egypt. At that time, the family size was about seventy-five persons. Approximately four hundred years transpired between that move (the end of Genesis) and the birth of Moses (beginning of Exodus) and much had changed including the size of the Israelite group who were fruitful and multiplied greatly and became exceedingly numerous.[1] At the time of the exodus, there were about six hundred thousand men on foot, besides women and children.[2] The total population including women and children has been estimated to be between 2,000,000[3] and 2,500,000.[4] This number was a concern to the Pharaoh at the time who worried if war breaks out, [they] will join our enemies, fight against us and leave the country.[5]

Consequently, Pharaoh ordered their oppression as slave labor, worked them ruthlessly[6] and ordered the killing of every boy born at the time of Moses's birth.[7] Moses survived this pogrom and came to the attention of the Pharaoh's daughter. Moses's birth mother cared for him and when he was weaned (the actual time with his mother was not recorded but thought to be two or three years[8] or more), he was returned to Pharaoh's daughter and he became her son.[9] He was educated in all the wisdom of the Egyptians and was powerful in speech and action.[10] Moses transitions from the son of a slave to royalty.

As with other historical events of several thousand years ago, there is some dispute concerning the historical period in which Moses lived. The exodus starting in or about 1445 BC "seems preferable in light of the fact that it is more faithful to Scripture, and provides a credible background for integrating the events of the exodus and conquest with Egyptian history and culture."[11] As Scripture identifies Moses as eighty years old when the exodus begins, Moses birth would have been in 1525 BC.

Neither the name of the Pharaoh nor is his daughter recorded in the Bible. Egyptian records contribute nothing to this either but placing the birth of Moses as indicated above as well as other know Egyptian events, suggests the Pharaoh's daughter may have been the future Queen Hatshepsut.[12]

The beginning of the exodus in 1445 BC also suggests Thutmose III was the Pharaoh when Moses fled to Midian (approximately 1485 BC) and his son Amenhotep II was Pharaoh at the start of the Israelite exodus. Egyptian influence at that time extended through the Palestine area to Mesopotamia. In 1457 BC, Thutmose III found himself faced with a coalition of the princes from Kadesh and Megiddo in Canaan, who had mobilized a large army. He attacked and successfully put down this rebellion in the Egyptian documented Battle of Megiddo.[13] This would have been approximately twelve years prior to the exodus.

There is no reference in the Bible of the Israelites fighting the Egyptians during their subsequent conquest of Canaan which started in 1405 BC. If holding their area of influence and the tribute it provided was so important to the Egyptians, why were they not involved? Because the Israelite exodus is not mentioned in Egyptian recorded history (it was not very complementary to the Pharaoh[14]), the defeat of Amenhotep II by the Israelites at the Red Sea may have been a deterrent to the Egyptians continuing the fight later.

The Exodus account skips ahead from Moses's birth to a time when he was forty years old[15] so little is actually known or recorded about Moses during these first forty years except that he was well educated for that time. In these ancient times, what would that education include?

Egyptian Education

Moses's formal education in Egypt was as extensive as available in this ancient world and would have included studies in reading, writing, languages, religion, architecture, mathematics, and sciences *as know at that time*. It may be difficult for us to image an education without all the sciences, mathematics, fine arts, philosophy, and literature we have available today but remember; this was about 3,500 years ago.

He would have learned such sports as archery and horseback riding which were favorite pastimes of a number of the Pharaohs of the Eighteenth Dynasty. He probably had opportunities to learn something of the languages of Canaan…as well as knowing the geography of that land.[16]

He most certainly took the Egyptian equivalent of the ROTC, studying the battles, combat tactics, and foes of that nation's proud military history. On top of that, he would have dabbled in the arts—sculpture, music, and painting. The whole world of Egyptian literature was opened to him. The adopted son of the princess found himself immersed in Egyptian learning. It became his life.[17]

What do we know of societal structure at that time and what might these studies have involved?

Societal Organization

In this twenty-first century, we are familiar with societal organization into countries, states, cities, etc. We are not as familiar with organization into tribes or city-states but such was the custom in the fifteenth century BC. The Israelites themselves were organized into twelve tribes that were descendant from the twelve sons of Jacob (Israel). Tribes were generally involved in hunting, were nomadic, or were practicing early forms of agriculture.

The first of the urban societies arose in Mesopotamia, between the Tigris and Euphrates rivers. Here the ancient Sumerian civilization flourished. Some time later in the Nile River valley the Egyptians developed their civilization.[18]

The Sumerian society developed city-states—each of which crowned a king as its leader. This was a stable society rooted in a single location and practicing animal husbandry or agriculture outside the city gates with commerce and significant population concentrations within the city. This form of societal organization spread into the region of Canaan as revealed by the large number of kings and their cities defeated by the Israelites in their later conquest.

The origins of ancient Egyptian civilization, which many regard as one of the fountainheads of Western culture, cannot be established with certainty. Archaeological evidence suggests that early dwellers in the Nile Valley were influenced by cultures of the Near East, but the degree of this influence is yet to be determined.[19]

Historical study recognizes that at some point, the dwellers of the low desert areas of southern Nile (Upper Egypt) were united as were the dwellers of the northern Nile (Lower Egypt) and these two were unified in approximately 3000 BC.

The ruling monarchs held absolute power over a strongly unified government. Religion played an important role; in fact, the government had evolved into a theocracy, wherein the pharaohs, as the rulers were called, were both absolute monarchs and, possibly, gods on earth.[20]

While the Israelites continued to be organized into tribes, their status changed from a nation of slaves in Egypt to a nation of nomads in the Exodus to that of land ownership similar to that of city-states when they conquered the region of Canaan.

Written Communications

The ideographic method of communication (pictures rather than words) may have been sufficient in the simpler societies of hunters and nomads. It could not, however, meet the needs of urban societies with their highly developed commerce, industry, agriculture, and state organization, all of which involved the need to keep records.

The people of Mesopotamia developed cuneiform, or wedge shaped impressions usually preserved in baked clay while the Egyptians developed a hieroglyphic form, which was a carefully drawn picture writing found mainly on public and official monuments. There were also hieratic and demotic forms, which were abbreviated, cursive writings used mainly for private and business correspondence.

Next in the history of writing was the syllabic stage. All syllabic writings were derived from the word-syllabic systems. They were either identical with or simplified from the syllabaries of those systems. A syllabary is a list of characters, each one of which is used to write a syllable.

The Babylonians and Assyrians, who superseded the Sumerians in the land of the Tigris and Euphrates, accepted almost without change the Sumerian word-syllabic system. The most radical changes took place in the system which the Semites of Syria and Palestine developed from the Egyptian word-syllabic writing between 1500–1000 BC.

The most important Semitic writing was developed around 1000 BC by the Phoenicians. Vowels were not included until the Greeks created the modern alphabet at a later date.[21]

Moses's education included the ability to read and write in a form that could convey ideas and thoughts much more complex that than available through pictures. This short history of writing also suggests that the writing of the first five books of the Bible may not have been possible much before the time of Moses.

Sciences

Most of what we understand today related to science was unavailable at the time of Moses. In the education of Moses around 1485 BC, science would have been limited to observations of the heavens (astronomy) and that was tied to religion. All earthly events and observations were thought to be a result of the actions of the gods. In our experience with scientific discovery involving very complex details of the nature of the universe, it is hard to place ourselves in the time of Moses where understanding was much more simplified. It is important to note that the place for science in the daily lives of people in that age was of little importance. Answering questions related to "how" events occur was much less important than questions related to "why." Astronomy is the study of celestial objects (sun, stars, planets, etc.) outside the earth's atmosphere.

> The earliest written records (i.e. history) were astronomical observations—Babylonians (~1600 BC) recorded position of planets, times of eclipses, etc…thus, Astronomy was the first science.[22]

> The annual flooding of the Nile was the foundation of Egyptian civilization and agriculture, so predicting this occurrence with accuracy was the driving force behind the development of Egyptian astronomy. Once again, their studies of the heavens became intertwined with religion, esoterica and the priesthood…There is little doubt that the great Egyptian buildings were based upon the stars; the Great Pyramid is aligned with the cardinal points, and many temples are aligned along the axis of the rising midwinter sun, signifying to Egyptians that they should begin to prepare for planting in the spring. The Great Pyramid of Giza is filled with astronomical significance, based largely upon religious beliefs but with its roots in astrological phenomena. Within the Great Pyramids are southern facing airshafts that point to the star Sirius, with its significance in marking the start of the Egyptian year, and to Orion, associated with death and rebirth, another recurring theme in Egyptian mythology. In addition, the north-facing air shafts point to the circumpolar stars, called 'The Immortals' by Egyptians, because they never set…The Egyptians built their monuments pointing in the cardinal directions and used them to reflect important celestial occurrences revealing the time of year. They also developed a sophisticated calendar.[23]

It wasn't until about the third century BC that the ancient Greeks were among the first to understand that the earth was a sphere in space, although the nature of that space was still misunderstood. Although ships were in use during Moses's time and the observation of the hull disappearing before the sails may have given some the idea of the curvature of the earth, no significant findings or study of this subject occurred until well after Moses's time.

As much of science known today starts with mathematics, its history may be of interest. While counting and arithmetic undoubtedly had their origins with a verbal language,

> The early history of mathematics is that of geometry and algebra.
>
> The first surviving examples of geometrical and algebraic calculations derive from Babylon and Egypt in about 1750 BC.
>
> Of the two, Babylon is far more advanced, with quite complex algebraic problems featuring on cuneiform tablets. A typical Babylonian math question will be expressed in geometrical terms, but the nature of its solution is essentially algebraic. Since the numerical system is unwieldy, with a base of 60, calculation depends largely on tables (sums already worked out, with the answer given for future use), and many such tables survive on the tablets.
>
> Egyptian mathematics is less sophisticated than that of Babylon but an entire papyrus on the subject survives. Known as the Rhind papyrus, it was copied from earlier sources by the scribe Ahmes in about 1550 BC.[24]

Thus, we see that although Moses may have had an introduction to simple geometry and algebra, mathematics was not well developed until well after the time of Moses.

The pyramids are one of the engineering wonders of the ancient world.

> The oldest known pyramidal in Egypt was built around 2630 BC…The last of the great pyramid builders was Pepy II (2278–2184 BC)… Later kings, of the 12th dynasty, would return to pyramid building during the so-called Middle Kingdom phase, but it was never on the same scale as the Great Pyramids. [25]

> Pyramid construction is a continuously debated topic. There are no existing records of building plans or discussions of construction methods, so no one knows exactly what happened.[26]

The sophistication of the surveying, excavation, orientation, quarrying stone, its transportation, and building the pyramids is amazing for that time in history. All the major pyramids would have been in place at the time of the Israelite exodus. Moses would likely have had at least some education in this engineering assuming that records were kept and survived the thousand years until Moses's education commenced.

Moses's world view would have been based upon the above understandings. It is not surprising that the first five books of the Bible contain little scientific understanding. There was little known about any of the sciences except observations from astronomy and basic mathematics at the time of Moses's education. It is not surprising that Moses could have written the books as the complex writing forms were known and likely included in his education.

Forty Years in Pharaoh's Court

The forty-year gap in the Exodus account of Moses from his birth to the next time he is mentioned covers considerable time for Moses. Whether he was three years old or older when he joined the daughter of Pharaoh, the early years would have been spent with his parents in the company of the Israelites. He was circumcised[27] in the tradition of his people and was undoubtedly indoctrinated into their religious faith. However, not much was known of God to His people other than perhaps the early human story and later His interactions with Abraham, Isaac, and Jacob. In fact, as we will see later, the Israelites were not yet "His people." If there were any other traditions, stories, or interactions with God that did occur, they would likely have been included by Moses when he wrote Genesis. To our knowledge in the biblical text, four hundred years had passed since the Israelite's last interaction with God! In fact, God says to Moses later on, "I have indeed seen the misery of my people in Egypt. I have heard them crying out because of their slave drivers, and I am concerned about their suffering. So I have come down to rescue them..."[28] So other than these traditions and understanding God's promise and covenant with their patriarchs, the Israelite understanding of God was limited. The apparent ease with which many of the Israelites later abandon their promises to God and worship idols suggest that their religion in Egypt may have also been influenced by the Egyptian beliefs as well as the other beliefs in the region.

Moses would have experienced an extreme swing in social activity moving from a slave encampment into the royal palaces of the Pharaoh and his daughter. His education and training would have consumed his time along with expected social interactions with other princes or princesses in the royal court. However, it is apparent that he never lost sight of his nationality. He knew his family who told him about his adoption (so he could write about it later) and knew his brother Aaron and sister Miriam.

Pharaoh was considered a god by the Egyptians. As a potential successor to Pharaoh, he could have become a god. Did he feel like a god? How did he feel about his heritage? Did he look down upon the Israelite slaves, as did the Pharaoh and his court? They were slaves while he was royalty. Did he feel a sort of survivor's guilt in why he was spared that life while others were not? Knowing the story of his birth, did he have guilt that he lived while other young boys may have been killed? (While we are informed of Pharaoh's order to kill baby boys, through the actions of midwives Shiphrah and Puah,[29] many were spared. Whether all boys survived the order is not known.) Although highly educated in the court of Pharaoh, did he really count himself an Egyptian? Perhaps he felt he didn't belong in either group and was totally isolated.

It is likely he had many questions about this but his personal contact and conversations with God did not occur until much later.

SECOND FORTY YEARS

Exodus 2:15 - 4:26

Loyalty

K nowing who he was, Moses would have been faced with an internal battle either to identify with the Egyptians or with the Israelites. As an Egyptian, he would have to watch and accept the brutal treatment of his own people. In the potential event he became Pharaoh, he might have eased their burden but with that large a slave population, it would have been difficult to remove their burden. In addition, he would have been worshipped as a god, so by faith, Moses, when he had grown up, refused to be known as the son of Pharaoh's daughter. He chose to be mistreated along with the people of God rather than to enjoy the pleasures of sin for a short time.[1]

This choice was put into action when one day, after Moses had grown up [forty years old],[2] he went out to where his own people were and watched them at their hard labor. He saw an Egyptian beating a Hebrew...Glancing this way and that and seeing no one, he killed the Egyptian...[3] This was a deliberate act and would be considered treason to the Egyptians. Inciting a rebellion with the Hebrews (Israelites) was the action that the Pharaoh feared. However, Moses thought that his own people would realize that God was using him to rescue them, but they did not.[4]

Moses clearly had not thought through his actions. If he had been considering instigating an uprising, he certainly would have made more preparations, including getting the backing of the Israelites. He was trained in military action which would have been required in an uprising but he was totally unprepared for this. Why he went out to watch them being mistreated and if these visits were a frequent occurrence is not known. Did he just get to the point that he could not stand it any longer? As Moses writes this passage, he does call them "his own people" so his mind-set at the time was to identify with them rather than the Egyptians. It has taken him forty years to come to this point so it must have been quite an internal struggle. However, in this rash action in killing the Egyptian, his own people reported his actions so that the act came directly to Pharaoh's attention. As a result, Moses fled to Midian.

Consider Moses's new internal struggle as he has rejected the royalty status offered by the Pharaoh to identify with the Israelites but these people have rejected him. He now has no one. He is alone.

Shepherd in Midian

Arriving in Midian, Moses married Zipporah, a daughter of Jethro (Reuel), the priest of Midian,[5] and tended his flock of sheep for the next forty years.

We can imagine the dejection and anguish Moses must have felt at this time. He left the palace of the Pharaoh to become a shepherd! Worse than that, four hundred years earlier, Moses's ancestor Joseph told his family that all shepherds are detestable to the Egyptians.[6] So Moses's new career was doing a job that his upbringing would have considered detestable. He had been so certain of his call to rescue his people only to be rejected by them. They even reported him to Pharaoh! Once a family member of the Pharaoh, he was now a hated man. What was his purpose in life after all that training and education? He has gone from an environment of high education and status with royal interactions to a lonely and singularly difficult job as shepherding sheep.

Moses's ancestor Jacob had a similar experience in working for his father-in-law Laban as a shepherd but with markedly different results. Jacob worked for Laban for about fourteen years and Jacob grew exceedingly prosperous and came to own large flocks, and maidservants and menservants, and camels and donkeys.[7] At the end of the next forty years, when Moses was eighty years old, he was still working the flock for his father-in-law. The Bible reports nothing of these forty years, but Moses doesn't show the ambition of Jacob and must have felt a humiliated and broken man.

Jethro is identified as a priest of Midian, but the Bible does not identify the god or gods he worshipped. As we will see later, the religion of the Midianites likely included several idols as well as God. This is supported later when Moses talks to Jethro following his calling and still later when Jethro meets Moses in the desert. Those events will be discussed later. Although Moses had been circumcised as a child, he did not circumcise his son[8] when with Jethro, so apparently, Jethro and Zipporah did not encourage it although they would have if they had been strict followers of the God of their ancestor Abraham. In addition, Moses must not have considered it important.

As an aside here, let's discuss Moses's family relationships. Prior to this time, his family as we know it, consisted of his mother and father (both of the tribe of Levi[9]), his older sister Miriam,[10] his older brother Aaron,[11] and the family he knew with his adopted mother, the daughter of Pharaoh. There is no mention of a wife or family in Egypt and such is unlikely since there are no companions fleeing Egypt with him or leaving later during the Exodus. This appears consistent with his identity confusion since he did not marry an Egyptian and marrying a slave would likely have ended his royal relationships. In Midian, he married Zipporah and has two sons identified as Gershom[12] and Eliezer.[13] There is some question whether Moses had married another, a "Cushite wife."[14] Cushite has also been translated as Ethiopian. It is unlikely that Moses married an Ethiopian while in Egypt for many reasons.[15] This will be revisited later.

God's Call to Moses

After forty years when Moses is now eighty years old, God calls to Moses from the burning bush near Horeb while Moses was tending the sheep far from his home. Moses recounts this event in Exodus chapters 3 and 4. Moses's first emotion is curiosity. He sees the burning bush but it is not consumed so he approaches it. God called to him, "Moses! Moses!" and Moses said, "Here I am."[16] God tells him not to come any closer and to remove his sandals for the place where he was standing was holy ground. God then introduces Himself as the "God of your father, the God of Abraham, the God of Isaac and the God of Jacob."[17] Moses now records his first real reaction to this event as hiding his face because he was afraid to look at God. It is my conjecture that Moses's education and lack of secure faith made this scene a curiosity and the last thing Moses expected was that this was a visit from God. Even if this was a spiritual event for Moses, it wasn't until God introduced Himself, thus separating Himself from all the many other gods of which Moses was familiar, that Moses reacted with fear of what might happen to him if he looked upon God. This is the God that his family would have talked about. This was not one of the gods of Egypt or the gods of the Midianites.

This is the first recorded encounter and conversation between God and Moses. Although no previous encounter is recorded, Moses believed that God aided his escape from Egypt in that he named his second son Eliezer for he said, "My father's God was my helper; he saved me from the sword of Pharaoh."[18] However, it is noted that Moses refers to "his father's [or ancestor's] God" and not his own.

As the author of Exodus, Moses certainly would have recorded any prior conversations had there been any but this encounter at the burning bush was totally unexpected. This was certainly a strange conversation. Moses doesn't want to do what God asks, argues with him, and finally says in effect, "Find someone else," which makes God angry.

Contrast this with a conversation Abraham has with God years earlier when God revealed His intent to punish Sodom and Gomorrah recorded in Genesis 18:20–33. Abraham is very careful not to anger God in his intercession for the righteous people that may be there. His speech is full of respect but Moses's tone doesn't show that respect.

Moses had become comfortable and secure with his life. He seemed satisfied with the role he was playing. Why would he want to go back to the life that so rejected him forty years earlier. Were these still his people? His wife was not an Israelite and they had turned against him before. Wouldn't they reject him again? There is no record that he had visited them at all for these forty years. Would he have even gone back to Egypt without the command of God? He even seems to invent an excuse for disobedience regarding his speaking ability. A speech impediment had not been revealed earlier and it does not appear to be an issue later on.

Probably acknowledging his own weak faith and the weak faith of the Israelites, Moses suggests the Israelites won't believe him when he tells them God sent him. After all, they didn't rally to him before. So Moses asks for signs to prove he is sent. Reluctantly, Moses accepts the assignment to go to Pharaoh to bring my people the Israelites out of Egypt.[19]

Speaking directly to God would be a "mountaintop" experience. People of religious faith generally eagerly relate such experiences with others of their faith. However, such experiences are difficult to explain or discuss with nonbelievers. Moses does not even mention his experience to Jethro but invents a reason to return to Egypt to see if any of his family is still alive. It is not until after the exodus from Egypt that Moses reveals to Jethro the direct contact with God and His demonstrated power. At that point, Jethro said, "Now I know that the Lord is greater than all other gods, for he did this to those who had treated Israel arrogantly."[20]

Moses takes his wife and two boys to travel to Egypt. Along the way, God makes it clear that although called by God, Moses needs to adhere to the requirements for all Israelites in circumcising their boys as part of their covenant relationship with Him.[21] Zipporah then performs the required actions but then, Zipporah and her sons leave Moses to return to Jethro[22] so again Moses is alone in his journey across the desert as he was forty years earlier.

These forty years of Moses's life end in a manner similar to the first forty: a significant transition in his life is in store, he is alone and he is entering unknown and uncertain circumstances. At this point, Moses has been introduced to God but still has not seen His power nor has the relationship developed yet to the point that Moses speaks to God as a friend.

BETWEEN EGYPT AND CANAAN

Exodus 4:27 - 40:38
Leviticus
Numbers 1:1 - 14:45

Moses and Pharaoh

When Moses returns to Egypt, he gains the support of the Israelites leaders and finally appears before Pharaoh. According to our accepted time line, Thutmose II would likely have been Pharaoh the last time Moses was in Egypt but in 1445 BC at the time of the first meeting, Amenhotep II (the son of Thutmose III and grandson of Thutmose II and Hatshepsut) likely was the Pharaoh. (Hatshepsut was the daughter of Thutmose I and half-sister to Thutmose II.) This is the same Hatshepsut who was identified earlier as the potential Egyptian "mother" of Moses. Hatshepsut and Thutmose III were deceased at the time Moses returns to Egypt, and it is likely that Amenhotep II was born during Moses's time in Midian. Thus, they would not have known each other except by reputation. It would seem unusual that Moses, as an Israelite and former traitor, would have access to the Pharaoh. Perhaps because Hatshepsut was Moses's "mother" and Amenhotep's grandmother and they were therefore related and that there were likely several royalty in the court who knew Moses and the history, Moses appears to have no difficulty gaining an audience with Pharaoh. In addition, those directly involved with his treason were dead. It also may be that Moses's previous experience in the court of Pharaoh eased this access to Pharaoh. We also know that after his first meeting with Pharaoh, God said to Moses, "See, I have made you like God to Pharaoh, and your brother Aaron will be your prophet."[1] God wanted these meetings and His will was that they proceed.

Regardless, Amenhotep II likely saw no great threat from Moses. In their first meeting, Moses took his brother Aaron with him and said This is what the Lord, the God of Israel says: 'Let my people go...[2] Pharaoh responds that he does not know this god and will not let the Israelites go. It is, however, likely that his education included information about God but he had no intimate knowledge or experience with Him.

Moses has the support of the Israelites in this first meeting with Pharaoh, but when Pharaoh increases the harsh treatment of the Israelites as a result, they quickly turn on Moses. Moses immediately complains to God that He is not helping them. God tells him that Moses will certainly see what God will do.[3] At this point also, none of the Israelites including Moses had seen any of the mighty works of God except Moses's experience with the burning bush.

Exodus chapters 5 through 12 record the plagues brought by God against Pharaoh until he finally relents and allows the Israelites to leave. These plagues and works are miraculous and mighty and show the power of God and the false power of the Egyptian gods including the Pharaoh who is unable to withstand these events. Pharaoh cannot stop the death of his own son.

After Pharaoh relents and lets the Israelites go, he later changes his mind and pursues them but is defeated by God at the Red Sea. With the Egyptian army approaching and their backs against the sea, the people forget the mighty acts of God that they have just seen and again complain to Moses. But this time, Moses's response is different. He reassures the Israelites that God will fight for them. The image of the water parting and piling up on either side of them as they walk through on dry ground is incredible. After the Israelites pass through the Red Sea, the Egyptians pursue them but God releases the water and the Egyptians are drowned. Then, when the Israelites saw the great power the Lord displayed against the Egyptians, the people feared the Lord and put their trust in him and in Moses his servant.[4]

This fear and awe was not long-lasting because when they encounter difficulties in the exodus, they grumble against Moses and God and often suggest they would be better off back in Egypt.

Shortly after leaving Egypt, the Israelites are attacked by the nomadic tribe of the Amalekites. Israel joins the battle and as long as Moses has his hands raised toward heaven, they prevail. While the Amalekites are defeated here, they are not totally destroyed and they will return periodically to attack Israel in years to come.

Three months after leaving Egypt, God leads the Israelites to Mount Sinai. Here Jethro, Moses's father-in-law, visits him and brings Moses his wife and two sons. Moses greets him and tells him all that God did for them in Egypt and Jethro is delighted to hear it. After providing some management advice to Moses concerning settling disputes, Jethro returns to Midian but Moses's wife and sons remain with Moses.

While at Mount Sinai, God provides the Ten Commandments, judgments and ordinances (the "Law"). It is here that He says, "Now if you obey me fully and keep my covenant, then out of all nations you will be my treasured possession."[5]

In the second year after leaving Egypt, God leads the people to Kadesh Barnea, near the promised land, and directs Moses to send in spies in preparation for their assault and conquest of the land. While the spies report how great this land was, ten of the twelve spies provide a scary image of the inhabitants and cause the Israelites to fear the battle. While two of the spies urge following God's direction, in the end the people refuse to attack. Because of this disobedience in the desert, God said, not one of the men who saw my glory and the miraculous signs I performed in Egypt and in the desert but who disobeyed me and tested me ten times—not one of them will ever see the land I promised on oath to their forefathers. No one who has treated me with contempt will ever see it.[6]

During these early months of the Exodus, God often spoke directly to Moses. The first conversations were directive in that God was providing instructions to Moses related to the ten commandments, building the tabernacle, the priesthood, religious holidays, and traditions and other instructions. Moses now has seen God's power and intentions and is at this point in a position to start having direct conversations with God. The nature of these conversations could have reflected Moses's initial interactions and that early relationship with God.

Who Are You, God?

It is likely all of us have asked this question and may still be asking it. God is always seeking us but most of us have a distinct recollection of our first real encounter with God. It may or may not have been as dramatic as Moses in seeing a burning but not consuming bush but God knows us well enough to know exactly how to get our attention. For Moses, it was his curiosity. For me, it was logic.

I was raised in a Christian home, but a personal faith could not be inherited. From an early age, I remember mathematics being my favorite subject. I was fortunate to earn my master's degree in mathematics, but my science and mathematics education drew me away from faith as had happened to many students entering college.

God never drew away from me; however, and soon after my marriage, my wife and I returned to church involvement. It was a couple of years later, in the midst of a building campaign that our pastor suggested we pray to ask God what we should commit. My logic had always led me to calculate what I should commit, but this time, we did pray independently; and having received the same response, we committed to this pledge on a Sunday.

The next Monday at work, a general pay increase was announced that matched exactly the commitment that we had made the day before. What are the odds or probability? Could this simply be a coincidence? I could not reconcile this event as anything other than God getting my attention. It was my burning bush. I, too, turned aside to look deeper into this mystery and thank God for His personal touch in my life.

Like many of us, Moses's first encounter with God appears to be a very confusing time for him. While he was curious, he was not fully committed to what followed. In fact, he initially shows little respect for God during this encounter. That, too, may sound like some of us.

It is supposed that the belief system Moses may have possessed at this time was a combination of the religions that he had been taught. Let us briefly explore this instruction.

The God of Abraham, Isaac, and Jacob

The book of Genesis records the history of God's relationship with man up to the start of Exodus. To this point, His relationship had been primarily with individuals. He said to Abraham, "Look up at the heavens and count the stars—if indeed you can count them... So shall your offspring be." Abram [Abraham] believed the Lord, and he credited it to him as righteousness[7] and the Lord made a covenant with Abram and said, "To your descendants I give this land, from the river of Egypt to the great river, the Euphrates."[8]

"I will establish my covenant as an everlasting covenant between me and you and your descendants after you for the generations to come, to be your God and the God of your descendants after you."[9] God confirmed his covenant with Isaac,[10] the son of Abraham and Sarah and also to Jacob, the son of Isaac.[11]

As a sign of this covenant, God said to Abraham, "Every male among you shall be circumcised…For the generations to come, every male among you who is eight days old must be circumcised."[12]

Abraham also fathered Ishmael, but God established the covenant with Isaac and his line. However, Ishmael was also circumcised.[13] At the time of the exodus from Egypt, all Israelite males had been circumcised.[14]

God is often referred to as the "God of Abraham and of Isaac and of Jacob." While Abraham had other descendants, God's covenant was with his son Isaac. Although Isaac had other offspring, God covenant was with his son Jacob. All of Jacob's descendants were included in God's covenant.

No interaction between God and any of the Israelites is recorded for the approximate four hundred years between their arrival in Egypt and the birth of Moses. While they had continued the practice of circumcision, the depth of their faith in the God of their fathers is unknown. They were immersed in a society that believed in numerous gods. We need to recall that God had not shown them any of his wonders and powers as yet and had not as yet provided His commandments. That would come during the exodus. Moses would likely have been taught the relationship of God with the Patriarchs (Abraham, Isaac, and Jacob) but it would not have been personal to him. Exodus records several times following God's demonstration of His power and salvation that the Hebrews grumbled against God and Moses about hardships along the way.

> The reaction of the Hebrews is quite typical of those whose spiritual perspectives are those which are conditioned by the present alone. Without a historical consciousness of what God has done and a deep-rooted faith in what God will do, one is easily moved by the emotion of a given situation.[15]

Egyptian Religion

The education of Moses certainly would have included an indoctrination into the Egyptian religious practices.

> Egyptian religious beliefs and practices were closely integrated into Egyptian society…

There were two essential foci of public religion: the king [Pharaoh] and the gods. Both are among the most characteristic features of Egyptian civilization. The king had a unique status between humanity and the gods, partook in the world of the gods, and constructed great, religiously motivated funerary monuments for his afterlife. Egyptian gods are renowned for their wide variety of forms, including animal forms and mixed forms with an animal head on a human body.

The Egyptians conceived of the cosmos as including the gods and the present world— whose centre was, of course, Egypt—and as being surrounded by the realm of disorder, from which order had arisen and to which it would finally revert. Disorder had to be kept at bay. The task of the king as the protagonist of human society was to retain the benevolence of the gods in maintaining order against disorder.[16]

As the son of Pharaoh's daughter, Moses could have been in-line to become a Pharaoh and thus could have himself become a god within the Egyptian religion.

Sumerian Religion

There was no centralized or organized set of gods for the Sumerians but rather each city-state had its own gods and priest-kings.

Each city housed a temple that was the seat of a major god in the Sumerian pantheon, as the gods controlled the powerful forces that often dictated a human's fate. The city leaders had a duty to please the town's patron deity, not only for the good will of that god or goddess, but also for the good will of the other deities in the council of gods. The priesthood initially held this role, and even after secular kings ascended to power, the clergy still held great authority through the interpretation of omens and dreams. Families also had their own special gods or goddesses...[17]

Abraham originally came from Haran in Mesopotamia and his grandson Jacob's wives Rachel and Leah also came from that territory. In their return to Jacob's father in Canaan, Rachel stole her father's "household gods"[18] evidencing the religious practices of the region.

Midian Religion

This religion will figure importantly in the spiritual development of Moses. The Midianites were descendants of Abraham through his wife Keturah.[19]

> The Midianites through their apparent religio-political connection with the Moabites are thought to have worshipped a multitude of gods, including Baal-peor and the Queen of Heaven, Ashteroth.[20]

While the Bible does not identify the specific religion of the Midianites, the above quote is supported in that Midian tried to destroy Israel during their time in the wilderness,[21] whom they should have known were God's chosen people.

Thus, at the time of the burning bush and into the initial months of their exodus, Moses would have been in the process of sorting out his religious priorities. He lived his first forty years with the gods of Egypt. He now has had a very personal encounter with God but his father-in-law was a priest for other gods and he lived forty years in this environment. He is the leader of the Israelites and following the instructions of God. But who is God, why is He most important and what about these other gods?

Let's listen in on the conversation.

Moses: You really got my attention Lord, with that burning bush. I knew of You before then but I thought You were one of many gods. I heard the faith stories of my parents, the Egyptians, Jethro, and others and understood there were many gods. Quite honestly, none of these stories made sense to me. I certainly was not a god but maybe something magically and spiritually changed if I became Pharaoh.

Moses, people get confused about the nature of spiritual things. Some deny any spiritual reality, others apply spiritual meaning to various objects I created and some make up their own ideas.

We knew of you but now have seen that you are more powerful than the Egyptian gods who could not stand up to you.

Moses, I am the first and I am the last; apart from Me there is no God.[22] Any mention of other gods are stories made up by people who are trying to explain things beyond their understanding or to provide justifications for the evil things they do.

Many times you have told us that you are the Lord our God. But in your commands you said "You shall have no other gods before me."[23] What about these other gods?

People will manufacture other gods that they will value and think or hope can help them. These may be physical images made of wood, silver or gold, but they are not real.

They have mouths, but they cannot speak, eyes, but cannot see. They have ears, but cannot hear, noses, but cannot smell. They have hands, but cannot feel, feet, but cannot walk, nor can they utter a sound with their throats. Those who make them will be like them, and so will all who trust in them.[24] They have no ability to do anything. They are nothing.

Some people may recognize the folly of these man-made objects but still substitute other things for Me. They may put their hope in wealth, which is so uncertain,[25] or amusements and entertainment, or the acclamation of men, or physical beauty. But woe to you who are rich, for you have already received your comfort. Woe to you who are well fed now, for you will go hungry. Woe to you who laugh now, for you will mourn and weep. Woe to you when everyone speaks well of you.[26] Woe to you if you value these as being more important than Me. There is nothing wrong with wealth or beauty alone, but these become "other gods" when people look to these things for their hope, happiness, or success rather than to Me.

I create you and give you your physical appearance. You have nothing to do with it so why would you boast about it. I provide you the ability to accumulate wealth and I own it all. It has no value for you once you die. You seek the favor of people and seek your own fame. Rather seek Me. These other things people worship have no concern for the people. They cannot provide what I am promising for you and the Israelites. These "other gods" will make your lives miserable and do not provide meaning or purpose. I bring you real life.

But you heard from many of these people that they felt they were better off without you. They have said many times that they should return to Egypt rather than suffer through this wilderness.

This is such a short-sighted reaction from a stiff-necked people. How quickly they forget their lives as slaves. On the other hand, I am the creator of life. I know what is good for you and what is in your best interest. My commands show you the better way. I have provided these commandments out of My love for You.

Still, I know many who will not accept You as their god.

That means then that they place themselves above me. I am the Lord; that is my name! I will not yield my glory to another.[27] I will not permit any other thing or person from taking my rightful place as God. I, the Lord your God, am a jealous God.[28] Those who do not accept Me have already made themselves a god in My place. They will be judged on the day of [My] wrath, when [my] righteous judgment will be revealed.[29]

Are they irredeemable, then?

No. [I] want all people to be saved and to come to a knowledge of the truth.[30] As surely as I live…I take no pleasure in the death of the wicked, but rather that they turn from their ways and live.[31]

I cannot understand how these people can actually see Your works and Your physical presence with us every day and still refuse to believe and trust You.

For this people's heart has become calloused; they hardly hear with their ears, and they have closed their eyes. Otherwise they might see with their eyes, hear with their ears, understand with their hearts and turn, and I would heal them. But blessed are your eyes because they see, and your ears because they hear.[32]

It's an understatement that when I first encountered You, I didn't want to be involved.

Some people are actually afraid to seek Me. Some are afraid that if they do find Me, their lives will change and they fear that. But I tell you ask and it will be given to you; seek and you will find; knock and the door will be opened to you. For everyone who asks receives; the one who seeks finds; and to the one who knocks, the door will be opened.[33]

Some are afraid to seek Me because they are evil. Everyone who does evil hates the light, and will not come into the light for fear that their deeds will be exposed.[34]

Some are afraid to seek Me because they may have done things of which they are ashamed, they regret it and think they are irredeemable. Godly sorrow brings repentance that leads to salvation and leaves no regret, but worldly sorrow brings death.[35] Their regret is a barrier to real life.

Lord, their resistance to You makes life very difficult for me and quite a source of discouragement. It makes no sense to me.

You are to proclaim…what [you] have seen and heard. I will help you speak and will teach you what to say.[36] Moses, you are not responsible for their faith or salvation. That is My work. Faith comes from hearing the message[37] and your job is to be obedient to me and to proclaim every command of the law to all the people.[38]

I don't always know the right words to use in proclaiming Your message.

You are to proclaim…what [you] have seen and heard.[39] I will help you speak and will teach you what to say.[40]

We all observed the plagues in Egypt and your defeat of Pharaoh's chariots. Your right hand, Lord, was majestic in power. Your right hand, Lord, shattered the enemy. In the greatness of your majesty you threw down those who opposed you. You unleashed your burning anger; it consumed them like stubble.[41] We are grateful that you chose us to be your people and not the Egyptians.

You have given us your commandments and warned us about what happens if we do not follow them exactly. We saw your wrath displayed against Aaron's sons Nadab and Abihu. Forgive me for being impudent here but is harshness your character?

You have much to learn about Me. I am the Rock, [My] works are perfect, and all [My] ways are just. [I am] a faithful God who does no wrong, upright and just [am I].[42] We'll talk of my justice later but while I am just, good and upright [am I]; therefore [I] instruct sinners in [My] ways. [I] guide the humble in what is right and teach them [My] way. All [My] ways…are loving and faithful toward those who keep the demands of [My] covenant.[43] Love is My character. I am love.[44]

At the same time I tell you, Among those who approach me I will show myself holy; in the sight of all the people I will be honored.[45] My just nature required consequences for people who disobey. However, there is still a blessing to be had here. Those who hope in [Me] will renew their strength. They will soar on wings like eagles; they will run and not grow weary, they will walk and not be faint.[46] We will talk later about what we are going to do here in the desert but they will know Me better through you and this experience together. It will also allow them to be witnesses to their children.

There are many who say that you were absent from our lives for more than four hundred years and even wonder whether the stories we were told about You before that were real. You created all things but many think You left us all alone after that.

When and where I choose to do things is up to Me. However, you have seen that "I have seen…have heard…came down…am concerned…"[47] These show I am always involved even though you may not have seen it. My presence now is with these people always in the smoke and fire. There will be a time when I am not with you in this visible way and many will again question my involvement but they will have your message and testimony on which they can rely and the message and testimony of their parents. Never will I leave you; never will I forsake you.[48] While I will never leave you, some of you will leave Me.

How will we remain with You if we cannot see You?

Through faith. The righteous person will live by his faithfulness.[49] Faith is confidence in what [you] hope for and assurance about what [you] do not see.[50]

While in Egypt, many of my people continued to believe that someday, You would fulfill the promise you made to Abraham. Others lived without this hope.

By faith Abraham, when [I] called [him] to go to a place he would later receive as his inheritance, obeyed and went, even though he did not know where he was going. By faith he made his home in the promised land like a stranger in a foreign country; he lived in tents, as did Isaac and Jacob, who were heirs with him of the same promise.[51]

But You were evident several times in Abraham's life. He certainly would have known You.

Yet I tested him in ways that would challenge his faith. Against all hope, Abraham in hope believed and so became the father of many nations… Even though he and Sarah were childless, I told him to look up at the sky and count the stars—if indeed you can count them…so shall your offspring be.[52] Without weakening in his faith, he faced the fact that his body was as good as dead—since he was about a hundred years old—and that Sarah's womb was also dead. Yet he did not waver through unbelief regarding [My] promise, but was strengthened in his faith and gave glory to [Me].[53] [Abraham] believed [Me], and [I] credited it to him as righteousness.[54]

How about those of us who don't see You or hear You like Abraham did? How do we hold faith in You?

Faith comes from hearing the message, and the message is heard through the word.[55]

This is one of the reasons I want you to write down all these things that are happening. Others will read and hear My message as recorded by you.

Lord, what we knew of gods was that they provided good things when we were good and bad when we were bad. Often we could not figure out why things were happening or why the gods were angry with us. Our religious leaders were supposed to intercede for us to keep order and keep on the gods' good side so that beneficial things would happen. Is that what I'm supposed to do with You?

It's not as simple as that. The gods you describe were fictions based upon superstition or convenience. They were given human traits and so could be filled with human failings and act in capricious ways. I am always good. I am clear about what I desire and it is good and for your good.

You are my chosen leader and set the example but you are not responsible for all the actions of the Israelites. Each is responsible for his or her own actions as you are responsible for yours. However, I will repay each person according to what they have done.[56] It may be immediate or it may be delayed at My will. I cause the sun to rise on the evil and the good, and send rain on the righteous and the unrighteous.[57] However, this is a big topic that we will save for a later time.

As to the benefits to the people, you saw My power displayed over the Egyptians on your behalf. When you were in the desert a short time and running low on food, I provided for your daily meals. When you were attacked by the Amalekites, I protected you. You do not need to be anxious about anything, but in every situation, by prayer and petition, with thanksgiving, present your requests to [Me].[58] I will sustain you. So do not fear, for I am with you; do not be dismayed, for I am your God. I will strengthen you and help you; I will uphold you with my righteous right hand.[59] You cannot yet grasp the blessings that come from my love nor have you yet come to understand my love. Love will always be my first choice.

I lived for eighty years not knowing You like this and I did not think my life was that bad. I know others that also were very surprised when You made Yourself known.

Moses, you did know me. For since the creation of the world, [My] invisible qualities…have been clearly seen, being understood from what has been made, so that people are without excuse.[60] All people have to do is look at this natural world to see Me. The heavens declare [My] glory; the skies proclaim the work of [My] hands.[61]

You are right that I did know of spiritual beings but didn't know it was You.

Then you did recognize that there is a higher power than you. You knew that you were not god. The knowing that there is a higher power influenced how you lived and raised your family.

There are some people who try to be and seem to be very good people who do not know you.

What do you know about what is good? There is only One who is good. If you want to enter life, keep [My] commandments.[62] Before I gave you My commandments, you had no standard of conduct by which to determine whether someone was acting properly or not. However, you knew in your heart what actions were acceptable and which were not. You did not need my command that You shall not steal[63] to know that it is wrong to take property belonging to another. However, some did steal and so violated a natural law. So, some "good" people may have lived in a way that you may not have known. For all have sinned and fall short of[64] [My] glory.

Are there no other spiritual beings than yourself? I know of the angels that serve you. They were present with Jacob and with Lot and his family.

Yes, Moses, there are other spiritual beings. Some, like the angels, serve Me. Others serve themselves or Satan. They will lead you away from Me.

Let no one be found among you who…practices divination or sorcery, interprets omens, engages in witchcraft, or casts spells or who is a medium or spiritist or who consults the dead.[65] These are the detestable things the inhabitants of Canaan are doing and you are not to do them.

I understand about some of this but is there harm in all of these things? Can they inform us of things we don't understand?

You don't need these practices. You have Me to lead you. You know that I love you and that I am working for your good. You are My people. I will not share you with any other being. They are not gods and will eventually lead you away from Me. The angels serve me. Do not worship them. Do not worship anything I have created. Worship Me.

There are no other gods so are you God only for the Israelites or are you God for all people? Is everyone else without any hope?

I am God for all people. I have chosen Abraham, Isaac, and Jacob's descendants as my people for now. You are my witnesses…and my servant whom I have chosen, so that you may know and believe me and understand that I am he. Before me no god was formed, nor will there be one after me.[66] [You, my people] will summon nations you know not, and nations you do not know will come running to you, because of [Me], the Holy One of Israel, for [I have] endowed you with splendor.[67] You will come to understand more fully, Who I am. You have much to learn about Me. We do have time for this on this journey.

Why Me, Lord?

How often have we wondered "Why me, Lord?" when asked to do something supporting God's work. We are often filled with excuses why we are not the right person and suggest someone else may be better suited. Moses is eighty years old and did not want the job of leading the Israelites out of Egypt. He argued with God that he was not the best choice. Who am I that I should go to Pharaoh and bring the Israelites out of Egypt?[68] Why then did God insist on Moses accepting this role?

Let's pick up on the conversation.

Moses: Lord, You know that I did not want to do what You asked of me. I was quite content with my life before knowing You and would have been content for it to continue that way.

You were resigned to your life but were you really content or happy, Moses?

Well, I thought I was happy. I had my family, extended family, and work. After forty years, it was my life and I was expecting it to remain as such. Was I really happy? I don't know that I ever really thought about that. What was the alternative for me? I was an outsider in Midian. But if I was content, why then did you confront me?

I have called you for My purposes.

Yes, but why did You chose me? I was eighty years old. That may be too old for this task.

I am the God of life. Your age is not important. Abraham and Sarah were already very old, and Sarah was past the age of childbearing[69] when I provided a son to them. With [Me], all things are possible.[70]

But, in my eighty years of life, I had accomplished nothing. I had a position once in Egypt but I blew it. When you called, I had no fame. No one knew me or respected me.

Moses, I knew you. I do not look at the things people look at. People look at the outward appearance, but [I] look at the heart.[71] I know what is in your heart.

I was not a good man. There are things in my past that I am not proud of. I did kill the Egyptian. I was a violent man, [You] showed me mercy because I acted in ignorance and unbelief.[72]

My grace is sufficient for you, for my power is made perfect in weakness.[73]

But those You have called in the past were great men. I do not fit in the same category as Abraham, Isaac or Jacob. Certainly, there are others who would have been a better choice.

They were not great men or perfect people before they knew Me. Each had his own shortcomings. However, Abraham believed [Me], and it was credited to him as righteousness.[74] I established my covenant with them and they believed Me and were obedient. Those were the character traits I value.

I am not qualified. I'm not a leader of people. The best I did was lead some sheep and I doubt Jethro even misses me as his caretaker.

In many cases, My people are like sheep without a shepherd.[75] Your training was valuable and My people will follow you.

Lord, I resisted you because I did not know what to say to Pharaoh or the Israelite leaders and was not eloquent. You said, "Who gave human beings their mouths? Who makes them deaf or mute? Who gives them sight or makes them blind? Is it not I, the Lord? Now go; I will help you speak and will teach you what to say."[76] You certainly did teach Aaron and me what to say.

Long ago I ordained it. In days of old I planned it; now I have brought it to pass.[77]

Lord, in my earlier days in Egypt I thought I would help my people. I tried to show them that I could help them overthrow their oppression. They did not believe or follow me then. At that time, I was sure I was doing the right thing. Why did You not help me then if it is the same thing I am doing now?

You thought you could do this on your own. I was not a part of your plan. You did not consult me. Unless the Lord builds the house, the builders labor in vain. Unless the Lord watches over the city, the guards stand watch in vain.[78] Your faith told you that you needed to choose the Israelites over the Egyptians but apart from me, you can do nothing.[79] I was with you but you would not be obedient to Me if you thought you could handle this on your own.

I think You have been with me since my birth. My parents told me of the wonder of my survival as a baby.

[I] created [your] inmost being; [I] knit [you] together in [your] mother's womb. [You are] fearfully and wonderfully made…[your] frame was not hidden from [Me] when [you were] made in the secret place…[My] eyes saw [your] unformed body; all the days ordained for [you] were written in [My] book before one of them came to be.[80]

If You had this in mind for me from my beginning, what then was the purpose of my life in Pharaoh's court?

Moses, see how I was with you even though you did not know it? It was My choice that you survive Pharaoh's attempt to kill you as an infant. I arranged for you to be found floating in the basket. You learned things in Pharaoh's house that have been and will be important for you in the days ahead. Your history in that house served you well when you had to ask Pharaoh to let My people go. You learned warfare skills. You learned communications and writing. You had experiences that helped equip you for your current role.

All that seemed so useless and such a waste of time while I was tending sheep in the desert.

That too was a time of development and growth for you. Not the way you planned but the way I planned.

I can see now that I needed to be humbled. It was quite a painful time. I often looked at the sheep and remembered the Pharaoh's court. I slept on the ground and remembered the soft beds in the palace. The sheep like to do their own thing but in Egypt, people obeyed my orders. Did you really need me to endure that for forty years?

Moses, I made a covenant with Abraham, Isaac, and Jacob that their descendants would inhabit the land I showed them. Surely, as I have planned, so it will be, and as I have purposed, so it will happen.[81] Several events needed to transpire before the time was right for you to go to Pharaoh. Not only did you need time to prepare, I was preparing Egypt for your return and the sin of the Amorites [had] not yet reached its full measure.[82] All is now ready.

Lord, I am beginning to know You. I realize now that You know me. I desire to trust You more fully and be obedient to You. Blessed are those you choose and bring near to live in your courts![83] Therefore, I ask: search me, God, and know my heart; test me and know my anxious thoughts. See if there is any offensive way in me, and lead me in the way everlasting.[84] Give me wisdom and knowledge, that I may lead this people, for who is able to govern this great people of yours?[85]

I don't know what lies ahead for me in leading these people to their Promised Land. I now know You will make this happen. I want to be with You and will do what You ask of me. You have been telling me, 'Lead these people,' but you have not let me know whom you will send with me… If you are pleased with me, teach me your ways so I may know you and continue to find favor with you.[86]

My Presence will go with you, and I will give you rest.[87]

We need you with us. How will anyone know that you are pleased with me and with your people unless you go with us?[88]

I will do the very thing you have asked, because I am pleased with you and I know you by name.[89]

One last thought on this, Moses. You resisted My call on you to this task but you should know that I do not call someone to action without providing the resources and support needed to accomplish the task. I will never leave you nor forsake you[90] as you carry out this assignment. Those who hope in the Lord will renew their strength. They will soar on wings like eagles; they will run and not grow weary, they will walk and not be faint.[91]

What Are You Doing?

How often do we ask "What does God want me to do?" While He may answer this directly, often a better question is "What is God doing and how can I help?" The first question focuses on us and we may get our desires in the way and the question changes to a prayer for God to bless what we want to do. The second question requires us to seek how God is moving around us and seeks to follow that direction.

Moses understood his mission from God was to lead the Israelites out of Egypt. While God did say He was going to bring them up out of that land into a good and spacious land, a land flowing with milk and honey[92] He did not show Moses that entire mission all at once. Nor did He show Moses his future plans at first.

Here is their conversation.

Moses: Lord, I know that You are leading us to the land You promised our forefathers. We were not trusting enough in You to fight for it when You directed. However, I do know that You will eventually do this. I suspect though that You have other objectives in mind.

You are correct that I will fulfill my promise to Abraham. I have indeed made his offspring numerous. I am not finished with that yet but I am also preparing these people to be My nation and for Me to be their God.

All the stories we heard were You leading individuals: Abraham, Isaac, Jacob, Joseph. We have not heard of You showing Yourself to many people at once.

It is time for Me to do a new thing. Long ago, I said to Abraham I have made you a father of many nations. I will make you very fruitful; I will make nations of you, and kings will come from you. I will establish my covenant as an everlasting covenant between me and you and your descendants after you for the generations to come, to be your God and the God of your descendants after you.[93] Now is the time for these descendants to know Me.

We knew some of what You did through the stories of our ancestors. But has any god ever tried to take for himself one nation out of another nation?[94]

I am doing a new thing. I am the Lord. I appeared to Abraham, to Isaac and to Jacob as God Almighty, but by my name the Lord I did not make myself fully known to them.[95]

I know that You showed favor on our forefathers and provided for them but we were unsure of what that meant for us these so many years later.

You have known of Me as the God of Abraham, Isaac and Jacob[96]— people that lived a long time ago. I am revealed now as the living and present God of all their descendants. I am now showing Myself as the God of all the Israelites. No longer will you refer to me in the past tense. I have given you commands for each individual to obey and for you as a nation to obey so that you will know Me personally.

You first revealed Yourself to us through the works You performed in Egypt by testings, by signs and wonders, by war, by a mighty hand and an outstretched arm, and by great and awesome deeds.[97]

People respect power. Whether the Egyptians or the Israelites, I showed My power to gain the attention of everyone. I said I will lay my hand on Egypt and with mighty acts of judgment I will bring out my divisions, my people the Israelites. And the Egyptians will know that I am the Lord when I stretch out my hand against Egypt and bring the Israelites out of it.[98]

We know full well that Your power is awesome and fearful.

I don't want you to be afraid of Me but to fear Me is to treat Me with awe and respect; with reverential trust. You should properly fear My wrath but you will also learn of My love. The fear of the Lord is the beginning of wisdom, and knowledge of the Holy One is understanding.[99] This is the beginning. Without Me, there is no wisdom, no understanding.

Why did you harden Pharaoh's heart? Why not just allow him to let us go?

It was not enough that Pharaoh let you go. Joseph was properly honored for his work in My name four hundred years ago. However, Egypt changed and mistreated My people. Their actions required punishment. I also wanted to show you and them Who I am and My power. It is something they will not soon forget as I plan for you to remember as well. The Israelites will also benefit from this in the future as they take the land from the current inhabitants. The inhabitants will have great respect for you because of My reputation. I have raised you up for this very purpose, that I might show you my power and that my name might be proclaimed in all the earth.[100]

We also saw that without You, we are unsuccessful. At Kadesh Barnea, we refused to obey you to enter the land. After You judged our actions, some then tried to fight against Your will and lost. We now have many years to wait before You will again lead us into this land.

I will bring you to the land I swore with uplifted hand to give to Abraham, to Isaac and to Jacob. I will give it to you as a possession. I am the Lord."[101] However, you now have to wait a bit longer. I brought you out from under the yoke of the Egyptians. I free[d] you from being slaves to them.[102]

What are we to do for these next many years while we wait for your judgment to be fulfilled?

The Israelites have been a nation of slaves. They have responded to the mistreatment by their masters. You will now become a free nation with My leading. They must learn obedience, not because of the whip but because of My promises and My love. You must also prepare yourselves as a nation to take the land I will give you. This will require military training and understanding—which you learned in Pharaoh's court. You too, Moses, have much to learn. For I know the plans I have for you, plans to prosper you and not to harm you, plans to give you hope and a future.[103]

You said that Your action in Egypt also was to show the Egyptians You are the Lord. Are you going to show all the nations who You are?

First, I will begin to put the terror and fear of you on all the nations under heaven. They will hear reports of you and will tremble and be in anguish because of you.[104] Observe [My commands] carefully, for this will show your wisdom and understanding to the nations, who will hear about all these decrees and say, "Surely this great nation is a wise and understanding people." What other nation is so great as to have their gods near them the way the Lord…is near [you]?[105] Though I will be known to them through you and My power displayed in your successes, the time is not yet fulfilled for all the nations. I did tell Abraham "through your offspring all nations on earth will be blessed, because you have obeyed me."[106] The blessing to all nations is still in the future and you and I will speak of this more at another time.

When the Israelites are ready to enter the land I am about to give them, they will be a united people; fully prepared to take on the responsibility and actions I will direct. They will celebrate victories in My name and enjoy life as I have prepared for them. Out of all nations you will be my treasured possession. Although the whole earth is mine, you will be for me a kingdom of priests and a holy nation.[107]

One last thought here, Moses: I am fulfilling a promise I made with Abraham, Isaac and Jacob. You must know that I am trustworthy in all [I] promise and faithful in all [I do].[108]

Images of God

Have you heard the stories of how the weathering of the side of a barn or the way a piece of bread was toasted produced an image that someone claimed was the face of Christ? These invariably draw crowds of people seeking this image. People look at Leonardo da Vinci's painting of "The Last Supper" and think it is historically correct including the images. It matters little that we have no real pictures of Jesus but only artists' paintings that were their own ideas. But the ease with which people latch onto such images illustrates the importance of this topic.

While Moses was on Mount Sinai for a long time receiving the Ten Commandments and instructions from God, the people grew impatient. They had promised just days before they would follow God and obey Him. Now they went to Aaron and said, "Come, make us gods who will go before us. As for this fellow Moses who brought us up out of Egypt, we don't know what has happened to him…"[109] He took what they handed him and made it into an idol cast in the shape of a calf, fashioning it with a tool. Then they said. "These are your gods, Israel, who brought you up out of Egypt."[110]

Moses certainly had further discussions with God on this subject. Perhaps it went like this.

Moses: Lord, let's talk about the golden calf.

My anger burned against the Israelites at that. I was ready to destroy them. Then I [was willing to] make you into a great nation.[111]

Yes, Lord. I have no desire to be separate from my people. I've been in that position before. I am a part of them and your actions with them are to me also.

But I see two separate sins in this golden calf incident. Your commandments were You shall have no other gods before me. You shall not make for yourself an image in the form of anything in heaven above or on the earth beneath or in the waters below. You shall not bow down to them or worship them.[112] Aaron had the image made and held worship there in honor of You, Lord. Others looked at the calf and proclaimed it as god in Your place.[113] The people's sin was against your command against other gods. Aaron's sin was against your command on making and worshipping images.

All who make idols are nothing, and the things they treasure are worthless. Those who would speak up for them are blind; they are ignorant, to their own shame. Who shapes a god and casts an idol, which can profit nothing? People who do that will be put to shame; such craftsmen are only human beings…He cut down cedars, or perhaps took a cypress or oak. It is used as fuel for burning; some of it he takes and warms himself, he kindles a fire and bakes bread. But he also fashions a god and worships it; he makes an idol and bows down to it. Half of the wood he burns in the fire…From the rest he makes a god, his idol…He prays to it and says, "Save me! You are my god!"[114]

The Egyptians have many gods and have many images that they have made to represent them. All the nations also have their images to worship. Why do people make images out of their own imagination to worship?

Just like the golden calf, people may make their idols either believing that the physical idol is their god or that it represents their god. For some who are spiritual, they find comfort in having a physical object to which they can direct their worship. Once established as an object of their worship, the physical object can become in their eyes the god they intend to worship. Like a scarecrow in a cucumber field, their idols cannot speak; they must be carried because they cannot walk. Do not fear them; they can do no harm nor can they do any good.[115]

Why then do people worship them?

There are uncertainties in life. In times of droughts or excessive rain, people may think they are being punished. In times of ample harvest, people may think they are being blessed. In times of challenge, worshippers of idols may think their idols can help them. In good times, worshippers may think they are pleasing their gods. They are seeking ways to keep on the good side of their god or of finding ways to explain things they do not or cannot understand. [I] will guide you always; [I] will satisfy your needs in a sun-scorched land and will strengthen your frame.[116]

What about good luck charms?

Some may take an object, such as a colorful stone, and believe it has good luck capabilities for them. Some may see an image in the clouds or in shadows that look like their god and worship that image. This is all nonsense. They have no power. You are to love the Lord your God with all your heart and with all your soul and with all your strength.[117]

There are some religions that promote actions directly against Your commandments.

You must not worship the Lord your God in their way, because in worshiping their gods, they do all kinds of detestable things [I] hate. They even burn their sons and daughters in the fire as sacrifices to their gods.[118] What evil thoughts and actions they promote! They prostitute themselves to their gods[119] and set up businesses to make money on these actions. This is all detestable to Me.

Some set up the worship rules for their own benefit.

Woe to those who call evil good and good evil, who put darkness for light and light for darkness, who put bitter for sweet and sweet for bitter. Woe to those who are wise in their own eyes and clever in their own sight.[120]

Why do You command no image for Yourself?

For my thoughts are not your thoughts, neither are your ways my ways.[121] Am I a calf? Am I a lion? Am I a bird? I created these things. You have no understanding of My image. [I am] spirit, and [My] worshipers must worship in the Spirit and in truth.[122]

Lord, I will tell the people: You saw no form of any kind the day the Lord spoke to you at Horeb out of the fire. Therefore watch yourselves very carefully, so that you do not become corrupt and make for yourselves an idol, an image of any shape, whether formed like a man or a woman, or like any animal on earth or any bird that flies in the air, or like any creature that moves along the ground or any fish in the waters below. And when you look up to the sky and see the sun, the moon and the stars—all the heavenly array—do not be enticed into bowing down to them and worshiping things the Lord your God has apportioned to all the nations under heaven.[123]

Moses, that is good. However, I have one more thought on this subject of my image. I created humankind in My image. So if all of you are in my image, regardless of complexion, height, personality, or other features, how could you possibly make a single image of Me?

Human Nature

The Israelites are called stiff-necked by God and by Moses several times during the exodus. (See Exodus 32:9, 33:5; Deuteronomy 9:6, 9:13, 10:16, 31:27). Stiff-necked refers to the Israelites as stubborn, haughty, prideful, arrogant, and resistant to God's and Moses's leadership. Are people today much different than those 3500 years ago?

Within a few days of the Israelites leaving Egypt, after they had seen the mighty miracles of God and with God's visible presence with them in the pillar of fire at night and pillar of cloud during the day, they see Pharaoh pursuing them and abandon hope in crying out to God and Moses: It would have been better for us to serve the Egyptians than to die in the desert.[124] Many times in the early wandering in the desert when faced with hardships or difficulties, the Israelites repeat this theme. They threaten Moses life and seek to rebel against Moses's leadership.

Perhaps their conversation went like this.

Moses: Moses bowed to the ground...and worshiped. "Lord," he said, "if I have found favor in your eyes, then let the Lord go with us. Although this is a stiff-necked people, forgive our wickedness and our sin, and take us as your inheritance."[125]

I have seen these people...and they are a stiff-necked people.[126]

Lord, why are these people so stiff-necked? They see you in the cloud and the fire. They heard you at Mount Sinai. Why do they so easily turn away?

Moses, it is not just the Israelites who are stiff-necked. Consider Adam and Eve. What was their first sin?

You told them not to eat fruit from the tree in the middle of the garden but when Eve saw that the fruit of the tree was good for food and pleasing to the eye, and also desirable for gaining wisdom, she took some and ate it. She also gave some to her husband, who was with her, and he ate it.[127]

Where did they get the idea that they would gain wisdom?

The serpent said that their eyes would be opened, and [they] will be like God.[128]

So, they were not willing to let Me be God but thought they could be like Me. It was this arrogance in them that drove them to want to be independent of me. They could then set their own rules. Life was very good for them before that. In fact, it was perfect, as I had created it to be.

So is it the serpent's fault that they sinned?

No. The serpent made the suggestion but it was their action. The suggestion would not have had any effect if they were solid in their obedience to Me.

You are saying that they had a choice available to them: whether to obey You or respond to the urging of the serpent. They chose incorrectly but You created them so that they could choose that way. Are You responsible for their fall?

Moses, I want all people to be saved and to come to a knowledge of the truth.[129] However, coming to that knowledge is for each person to experience. I provided people with free will. That is, I did not create them as pets or domesticated animals that I lead by a ring through the nose. I desire a relationship with all people but there is no relationship without a two-way commitment. I do not want obedience and respect because they have no choice or options but because through faith, the people believe in Me and want that relationship.

Didn't you really set them up to fail? Did you have to make the fruit of the tree enticing?

I provided a test of their obedience. I suppose I could have said everything was permissible except to cut off one's little finger but the test had to provide a true choice. There was plenty of other desirable fruit in that garden.

But You told me that You hardened Pharaoh's heart against You. That was Your choice. Did you cause Adam and Eve to sin also?

Adam and Eve made their own choice. When tempted, no one should say, "God is tempting me." For [I] cannot be tempted by evil, nor do [I] tempt anyone; but each person is tempted when they are dragged away by their own evil desire and enticed. Then, after desire has conceived, it gives birth to sin; and sin, when it is full-grown, gives birth to death.[130] Adam and Eve's sin started with their arrogance in believing that they didn't need to be obedient to me and that through the action of disobedience, they could be god in My place. That led to their action and ultimate separation from Me. As for Pharaoh, I have many purposes in mind. I know the outcomes for My actions and because I am the Creator, all things belong to Me, including Pharaoh. You do not know the reasons why I do things nor will I necessarily explain them to you. You also do not know all the results of My actions.

For me, your place as my God is secure because I talk with You. I've seen You in action and know of Your power and authority.

Moses, you were a bit rebellious against Me when we first met, were you not? Adam and Eve had this same relationship. I walked and talked with them daily.

Maybe I was a bit stiff-necked also then. So I guess all mankind runs the risk of disobedience and rejecting You.

As I say, Moses, I desire that all would want a lasting and fulfilling relationship with Me. They need nothing more.

The penalties for disobeying You can be very severe. For Adam and Eve, it changed forever our relationship with You, each other and with Your creation.

I am a just God. That means that I cannot simply overlook sin and disobedience. It would be unjust to do so. So you must endure hardship as discipline; [I am] treating you as [My] children. For what children are not disciplined by their father? If you are not disciplined—and everyone undergoes discipline—then you are not legitimate, not true sons and daughters at all...Moreover, [you] have all had human fathers who disciplined [you] and [you] respected them for it...They disciplined [you] for a little while as they thought best; but [I] discipline [you] for [your] good, in order that [you] may share in [My] holiness. No discipline seems pleasant at the time, but painful. Later on, however, it produces a harvest of righteousness and peace for those who have been trained by it.[131]

You have promised great rewards for obeying You.

There are so many blessings I can bestow on those who love me and seek me. This is what I desire to do. Keep [My] decrees and commands...so that it may go well with you and your children after you and that you may live long in the land [that I] give you for all time.[132] [I] will make you most prosperous in all the work of your hands and in the fruit of your womb, the young of your livestock and the crops of your land. [I] will again delight in you and make you prosperous, just as [I] delighted in your ancestors, if you obey the Lord your God and keep [My] commands and decrees that are written in this Book of the Law and turn to [Me] with all your heart and with all your soul.[133]

If you follow My decrees and are careful to obey My commands, I will send you rain in its season, and the ground will yield its crops and the trees their fruit. Your threshing will continue until grape harvest and the grape harvest will continue until planting, and you will eat all the food you want and live in safety in your land.

I will grant peace in the land, and you will lie down and no one will make you afraid. I will remove wild beasts from the land, and the sword will not pass through your country. You will pursue your enemies, and they will fall by the sword before you. Five of you will chase a hundred, and a hundred of you will chase ten thousand, and your enemies will fall by the sword before you.

I will look on you with favor and make you fruitful and increase your numbers, and I will keep my covenant with you. You will still be eating last year's harvest when you will have to move it out to make room for the new. I will put My dwelling place among you, and I will not abhor you. I will walk among you and be your God, and you will be My people. I am the Lord your God, who brought you out of Egypt so that you would no longer be slaves to the Egyptians; I broke the bars of your yoke and enabled you to walk with heads held high.[134]

You made us in Your image. Isn't it then part of our nature to want to be like You?

Yes, you should want to be like Me. I desire that you want to be with Me and worship Me and fear and love Me but not to take My place as your God.

How then are we made in Your image?

In the beginning, I said, let us make mankind in our image, in our likeness…So [I] created mankind in [My] own image, in the image of God [I] created them; male and female [I] created them.[135] I am spirit and you are spirit as well. You have a physical body and I too can be a physical being. I have instilled in you a bit of who I am. You have seen My creativity—the wonders of this world and the varieties of animals and people. I have given each of you a bit of My creativity. When you sing, when you dance, when you plan, when you write, when you study the heavens, when you dream, when you work with skill with gold or silver, when you laugh, when you love… these are all part of who I am. But you are incomplete without Me. Being in My image means that you have a longing to be with Me whether you recognize it or not.

I tended those sheep for forty years but did not recognize them as being part of You nor my "skill" as anything resembling Your creativity. Not once did I see watching and leading them as being related to what You are.

Moses, there can be joy in doing all types of work. Whatever you do, work at it with all your heart, as working for [Me], not for human masters, since you know that you will receive an inheritance from [Me] as a reward. It is [Me] you are serving.[136]

I do have some abilities but don't have all the skills or gifts you mentioned.

None of you can do or be all of these things but you do have your own set of skills and abilities that I have given you. Use them in My service.

Some of us have greater skills and abilities than others. You know I don't think much of my speaking ability.

You should not judge your ability against another. As long as each of you apply your abilities as I have assigned, your nation will have sufficient skill and ability to complete what I have in mind. You all belong as parts of a body. Now if the foot should say, "Because I am not a hand, I do not belong to the body," it would not for that reason stop being part of the body. And if the ear should say, "Because I am not an eye, I do not belong to the body," it would not for that reason stop being part of the body. If the whole body were an eye, where would the sense of hearing be? If the whole body were an ear, where would the sense of smell be? But in fact [I have] placed the parts in the body, every one of them, just as [I] wanted them to be. If they were all one part, where would the body be? As it is, there are many parts, but one body.[137]

That brings me back to the question of why some of us refuse to obey You or even acknowledge You. They are not acting as part of the body. What would it take for them to see and understand?

Moses, they have seen and refuse to believe. I did wondrous signs in Egypt—signs and actions they could not. But did that convince them? No. I am all around you. All you need is faith and your eyes will see. Without faith, one cannot see even when I am right in front of them.

But where does faith come from? How can we help those who do not have faith?

Faith comes from Me. For it is by grace you have been saved, through faith—and this is not from yourselves, it is [My] gift—not by works, so that no one can boast.[138] You are not saved by what you do but by your faith. And this faith is my gift to you.

You mean that if one does not have faith to believe, it is because You did not give him that faith?

We are back to free will. Ask and it will be given to you; seek and you will find; knock and the door will be opened to you. For everyone who asks receives; the one who seeks finds; and to the one who knocks, the door will be opened.[139] One who truly seeks Me will find Me and I will provide the gift of faith. What good would this gift be to those who refuse to accept it? Not all the Israelites accepted the good news…Consequently, faith comes from hearing the message.[140] But one must be open to hearing this message clearly.

While we have no image of You, You are with us every day and we see Your presence in the fire and the cloud. Will You always show yourself in this way?

GOD—MOSES—ME

No. I am with you now in this way while my people are on this journey. Once they are ready to enter the land I promised on oath to Abraham, I will no longer be visible this way. Then they are to continue to worship me as I have commanded. I will establish a place for my name there to be a center for my worship.

Lord, these are a stiff-necked people. They will depart from Your commands when You are not visible to them.

They must be taught my ways. These commandments that I give you… are to be on your hearts. Impress them on your children. Talk about them when you sit at home and when you walk along the road, when you lie down and when you get up.[141] As for you and this generation, because you have seen me, you have believed; blessed are those who have not seen and yet have believed.[142]

The rituals, the celebrations, and holidays I have directed are important for you, as is the record of these events I have directed you to write. When I am unseen, the people must remember these events and relive them frequently in order to sustain their faith. I will continue to show myself to them at proper times to strengthen this faith. The fear of the Lord is the beginning of knowledge, but fools despise wisdom and instruction.[143]

There are some who suggest that the works You performed were actually naturally occurring events. Without direct physical proof, they may not believe in You. When You parted the sea with that wind, some say that was a naturally occurring wind.

A wind that just happened to occur when you needed it? A wind that was strong enough to pile up the water but not blow away all the people walking through on dry land? What proof could be acceptable to them? The Lord sitting on a throne or leading the battle? No one can see my glory and live. Any other physical image would certainly result in attempts to make idols representing me. [You] live by faith, not by sight.[144] For it is with your heart that you believe and are justified, and it is with your mouth that you profess your faith and are saved.[145]

Are you ever going to make Your presence known so well that all cannot refuse to believe?

Moses, any physical evidence that I could provide would be discounted by those without faith just as parting the sea. If I created a cylindrical rock structure 300 cubits high (approximately 450 feet), they would assume that

44

others chiseled this structure out of rock and carried off the debris. Even so, if there were irrefutable proof, there would be no need for faith.

So some of us who saw Your miracles will discount them.

Yes, in their desire to rid themselves of Me, they will deny the power of the miracles or their source.

What then is the purpose of miracles?

You are to write down all these events. Those of you who saw them are to tell their children. This will be a witness to future generations. While those who saw these things will not enter the promised land, they will be eye-witnesses to their children. The children then can tell their children that their grandparents were eye-witnesses and so forth through the years. The festivals, these stories and your written book will provide strength to the faith of My people. They are not the only source of faith but will help to provide pillars in the faith that they may lean on when required. The miracles do not produce faith but provide the opportunity for faith to grow for those who are open or seeking that faith.

Because we are stiff-necked and short sighted, we will need to see you in action from time to time. I have told these people, For I know how rebellious and stiff-necked you are. If you have been rebellious against the Lord while I am still alive and with you, how much more will you rebel after I die!…For I know that after my death you are sure to become utterly corrupt and to turn from the way I have commanded you.[146] We cannot survive without You and Your presence.

I will be with those who seek Me throughout the ages. I will reveal Myself to them in many ways. At the proper time, I will send another to you who will be in My image and represent me to all the people.

Lord, Although this is a stiff-necked people, forgive our wickedness and our sin, and take us as your inheritance.[147]

The Ten Commandments

The Ten Commandments are often a point of contention between religious and nonreligious people. Often the argument on one side is that the separation of church and state makes the Ten Commandments only a religious topic and therefore should not be part of any public place. On the other side, religious people say that God's law is foundational in our understanding of law and should guide our actions. However, even on the religious side, protestant Christian churches may not agree on how to number or group the ten commandments and Jewish leaders consider that these may be ten topics of an even larger number of commandments. Some think that since these are in the Old Testament, they no longer apply to Christians.

On Mount Sinai, God said to the Israelites, "Now if you obey me fully and keep my covenant, then out of all nations you will be my treasured possession."[148]

> A careful study of both Old and New Testament will reveal the fact that the Law had a five-fold purpose in the plan of God. (1) It was designed to reveal man's sinfulness (Rom. 3:19–20). (2) It uncovered or illustrated the hideous nature of sin (Rom. 7:8–13). (3) It revealed the holiness of God. (4) It restrained the sinner so as to help him to come to Christ (Gal. 3:24). (5) It restrained wrong behavior so as to protect the integrity of the moral and social and religious institutions of Israel.[149]

While there are generally accepted norms of behavior (i.e., we do not take another's property without permission) until God provided the law, the Israelites had no standard for behavior. One could not technically be guilty of sin by committing adultery until God established that it was law. It therefore revealed man's sinfulness and informed the believer of God's standard of behavior.

Recall that when God gave the Israelites the law, Christ's birth, crucifixion and resurrection were still 1400 years in the future. Through Jesus' sacrifice and substitutional death for our sins, believers live under God's grace and are not judged by obedience to the law.

> The New Testament makes it very clear that the child of God living in the Age of Grace is not under law and not obligated to the Mosaic code as was the Israelite under the old economy… The means of salvation for men in all ages has been faith…The difference then is not in salvation, but the means by which one's conduct is governed.[150]

In addition to the Ten Commandments providing God's plan, it also provides a testament of His love for His people. God created us and as He is perfect, He knows what behavior is in our own best interests. If we live in accordance with His plan, we can avoid so many of the causes of pain and suffering we experience. The Law provides His plan for how we are to relate to Him and others.

Moses certainly had conversations with God on so important a topic as God's commands. This might be how it unfolded.

Moses: Lord, I would like to talk about Your law and what it means for us. You gave us a lot of rules in a very short time. This is a lot to consider.

Since I am your God and you are my people, you need to know how I expect you to behave. We need to start right now. Your old way of life is no longer acceptable. When you entered your military training in Egypt, your life changed immediately. There was no gradual change to the military way of life. So it is here. The people need to know Me and My rules for life.

These laws direct us mostly in behavior we are to avoid. Do You intend it to be direction for what we are to do?

Love the Lord your God with all your heart and with all your soul and with all your mind…Love your neighbor as yourself. All the Law…hang on these two commandments.[151]

These commandments tell you what not to do and what you should do to relate to Me and to others.

We talked before about You being the only God and we are to honor You above all things. We also talked about Your command against making images.

You then said, "You shall not misuse the name of the Lord your God."[152] In what way would we misuse Your name?

You may swear by My name but My name is holy. If you swear by My name, you must tell the truth. Do not swear falsely by my name and so profane the name of your God. I am the Lord.[153] Do not curse, swear, or casually use My name in any way other than in reverence and respect. Do not profane my holy name.[154] Use my name in prayer, praise, and thanksgiving.

You said, "Remember the Sabbath day by keeping it holy. Six days you shall labor and do all your work, but the seventh day is a sabbath to the Lord your God."[155]

You also told us to gather the manna six days but not to look for it or try to gather it on the Sabbath. Why is this important to you?

I worked for six days during my creation activity, but by the seventh day [I] had finished the work [I] had been doing; so on the seventh day [I] rested from all [My] work. Then [I] blessed the seventh day and made it holy, because on it [I] rested from all the work of creating that [I] had done.[156] This is a very special time for Me.

On it you shall not do any work, neither you nor your son or daughter, nor your male or female servant, nor your ox, your donkey or any of your animals, nor any foreigner residing in your towns, so that your male and female servants may rest, as you do.[157] It is important for you to have a day of rest. Your lives are busy and in the rush of activities, it is necessary to purposefully take time off and restore your well-being.

This is also a sign of obedience to My command. If you keep your feet from breaking the Sabbath and from doing as you please on my holy day, if you call the Sabbath a delight and the Lord's holy day honorable, and if you honor it by not going your own way and not doing as you please or speaking idle words, then you will find your joy in the Lord, and I will cause you to ride in triumph on the heights of the land and to feast on the inheritance of your father Jacob.[158]

While I want a continuous relationship with you, the Sabbath provides you time to specifically think about Me and worship Me. This helps keep Me the focus of your lives. This should be a time of teaching of My promises and commands and eager hearing of this message. It is time to reflect on what I have done and who I am. It is a time that parents may provide instruction to their children and demonstrate their devotion to Me. Of course, you can do this on all days and I desire that. However, designating a specific day for this time of worship and reflection helps you take your focus off the troubles and issues of your day and look to Me and My promises to care for you.

You said, "Honor your father and your mother, so that you may live long in the land the Lord your God is giving you."[159]

Why are You purposefully calling us to honor our parents?

The relationship between parents and their children is especially important and significantly impactful in all human interactions. Conflict in this relationship can be a source of great anxiety. Often this starts over issues occurring during the growth and maturity of children. While I expect all people to love one another, I am specifically calling on children to show love, honor, respect, and esteem for their parents. Of course, the parents are to love and honor their children and not provoke them. Every father must manage his own family well and see that his children obey him, and he must do so in a manner worthy of full respect.[160] When parents age and require greater support, the children will retain this responsibility to care for them. In this way, children's children are a crown to the aged, and parents are the pride of their children.[161]

Tell the people to listen to your father, who gave you life, and do not despise your mother when she is old…The father of a righteous child has great joy; a man who fathers a wise son rejoices in him.[162]

Because I am your Father, I also equate your honoring of your earthly parents as part of your honoring Me.

You said, "You shall not murder."[163]

Moses, I formed a man from the dust of the ground and breathed into his nostrils the breath of life, and the man became a living being.[164] Life belongs to me. It is mine alone to handle. There is no god besides me. I put to death and I bring to life, I have wounded and I will heal.[165] Unless I direct you otherwise, you are not to take the life of my people. You are to protect life especially for those who are unable to protect themselves. I look for those who say, I rescued the poor who cried for help, and the fatherless who had none to assist them.[166]

Even more, I say that you are not to do any bodily harm to anyone. Do not do anything that endangers your neighbor's life. I am the Lord. Do not hate a fellow Israelite in your heart.[167] Likewise, anyone who is angry with a brother or sister will be subject to judgment. And anyone who says, 'You fool!' will be in danger of the fire of hell.[168] Whoever mocks the poor shows contempt for their Maker; whoever gloats over disaster will not go unpunished.[169]

Not only should you be protectors of life, you should be helpful to preserve life and assist others in their every need.

You said, "You shall not commit adultery."[170]

Moses, I designed and created life including the means for procreation. I gave you the gift of sex and designed it so that it is a special union of a man and a woman. A man will leave his father and mother and be united to his wife, and the two will become one flesh. So they are no longer two, but one flesh. Therefore what God has joined together, let no one separate.[171]

By "no one," I also mean that man and that woman themselves. If you are married, sexual relations with someone not your husband or wife or sexual relations with a husband or wife of another is adultery. Everyone is hurt by this action, relationships are broken, and this special union created in marriage is damaged.

> My son, pay attention to my wisdom, turn your ear to my words of insight, that you may maintain discretion and your lips may preserve knowledge.
>
> For the lips of the adulterous woman drip honey, and her speech is smoother than oil; but in the end she is bitter as gall, sharp as a double-edged sword.
>
> Her feet go down to death; her steps lead straight to the grave. She gives no thought to the way of life; her paths wander aimlessly, but she does not know it.[172]

Adultery is not only in the mind and actions of a woman but also of a man. But I tell you that anyone who looks at a woman lustfully has already committed adultery with her in his heart.[173]

Moses, a married couple is to love and honor each other; to mutually build each other up. They are to care for each other, respect each other, support each other.

Love is patient, love is kind. It does not envy, it does not boast, it is not proud. It does not dishonor others, it is not self-seeking, it is not easily angered, it keeps no record of wrongs. Love does not delight in evil but rejoices with the truth. It always protects, always trusts, always hopes, always perseveres.[174]

> Drink water from your own cistern, running water from your own well.

> Should your springs overflow in the streets, your streams of water in the public squares?
>
> Let them be yours alone, never to be shared with strangers.
>
> May your fountain be blessed, and may you rejoice in the wife of your youth.[175]

You said, "You shall not steal."[176]

Moses, I have provided all people with the ability to work and obtain the necessities of life. It does require effort. All hard work brings a profit, but mere talk leads only to poverty.[177]

I am the Great Provider. I will provide for all your needs. It is not necessary for you to take from someone else. Therefore I tell you, do not worry about your life, what you will eat or drink; or about your body, what you will wear. Is not life more than food, and the body more than clothes? Look at the birds of the air; they do not sow or reap or store away in barns, and yet [I] feed them. Are you not much more valuable than they? I know what you need and will provide.

> All creatures look to [Me] to give them their food at the proper time.
>
> When [I] give it to them, they gather it up; when [I] open [My] hand, they are satisfied with good things.[178]

For those truly in need, you are to assist them. This is one way I desire to provide for their needs. But when you give to the needy, do not let your left hand know what your right hand is doing, so that your giving may be in secret. Then [I], who sees what is done in secret, will reward you.[179]

Be aware that whoever loves money never has enough; whoever loves wealth is never satisfied with their income.[180]

Each is to be satisfied with what they have or work to earn what they want. Stealing comes from coveting what others have and you do not.

Do not defraud or rob your neighbor. Do not hold back the wages of a hired worker.[181] What I am also telling you in the command is that contrary to stealing, which takes from someone else, you are to assist others in keeping their possessions and to help others improve and protect their possessions and means of earning a living. Do nothing out of selfish ambition or vain conceit. Rather, in humility value others above yourselves, not looking to your own interests but each of you to the interests of the others.[182]

You said, "You shall not give false testimony against your neighbor."[183]

Do not go about spreading slander among your people.[184] Do not spread false reports. Do not help a guilty person by being a malicious witness.[185]

I am telling you to live with integrity. Do not adjust your testimony to serve your own needs or to see an outcome that you desire.

Do not pervert justice; do not show partiality to the poor or favoritism to the great, but judge your neighbor fairly.[186]

Do not follow the crowd in doing wrong…do not pervert justice by siding with the crowd.[187]

You are responsible for what you say.

You are to care for each other. Do not deny justice to your poor people… do not accept a bribe.[188]

Therefore encourage one another and build each other up…encourage the disheartened, help the weak, be patient with everyone.[189]

Therefore each of you must put off falsehood and speak truthfully to your neighbor…Do not let any unwholesome talk come out of your mouths, but only what is helpful for building others up according to their needs, that it may benefit those who listen. Get rid of all bitterness, rage and anger, brawling and slander, along with every form of malice. Be kind and compassionate to one another, forgiving each other.[190]

You said, "You shall not covet your neighbor's house. You shall not covet your neighbor's wife, or his male or female servant, his ox or donkey, or anything that belongs to your neighbor."[191]

Be satisfied with what you have.

A heart at peace gives life to the body, but envy rots the bones.[192] But godliness with contentment is great gain.[193]

Work honestly for what you have and desire.

Watch out! Be on your guard against all kinds of greed; life does not consist in an abundance of possessions.[194]

Death and Destruction are never satisfied, and neither are human eyes.[195]

You should not look with envy at what your neighbor has but rejoice with him over what he has. Help him to enjoy it and keep it. If you are in need, do not be anxious about anything, but in every situation, by prayer and petition, with thanksgiving, present your requests to God.[196]

If you live with respect and care for others,

> If you do away with the yoke of oppression, with the pointing finger and malicious talk, and if you spend yourselves in behalf of the hungry and satisfy the needs of the oppressed, then your light will rise in the darkness, and your night will become like the noonday. The Lord will guide you always; he will satisfy your needs in a sunscorched land and will strengthen your frame. You will be like a well-watered garden, like a spring whose waters never fail[197]

As we try to keep your commands, I know you have given us promises as our God.

Put to death, therefore, whatever belongs to your earthly nature: sexual immorality, impurity, lust, evil desires and greed, which is idolatry…But now you must also rid yourselves of all such things as these: anger, rage, malice, slander, and filthy language from your lips. Do not lie to each other…Therefore, as God's chosen people, holy and dearly loved, clothe yourselves with compassion, kindness, humility, gentleness and patience. Bear with each other and forgive one another if any of you has a grievance against someone. Forgive as the Lord forgave you. And over all these virtues put on love, which binds them all together in perfect unity.[198]

Set your minds on things above, not on earthly things.[199] Finally, brothers and sisters, whatever is true, whatever is noble, whatever is right, whatever is pure, whatever is lovely, whatever is admirable—if anything is excellent or praiseworthy—think about such things.[200]

Relating with God

How do we describe our relationship with God? If there is a God in heaven, does He care about me personally or all of us collectively? Does He know me and can I know Him? Does He want us to find a spokesperson to be our go-between? Can we reach Him on our own? Do we want to reach Him?

I would suspect Moses had these questions before his first encounter with God. I think he would have addressed this topic directly—perhaps as follows.

Moses: Lord, I have a very unique relationship with You. I speak with You plainly and directly. You speak to me very clearly. The rest of the people have told me that they want me to be a spokesman for You. They told me do not have God speak to us or we will die.[201] I love this relationship with you but what about the rest of the people? How can they relate directly with You?

Moses, I want all to relate to me both individually and corporately. I have provided holidays and commands for the whole community. At the same time, I have provided commands for individuals to obey. I desire that My relationship with each person be as real and individual as they are. As a people and as individuals, you are to be and in fact, are different from all other peoples on the earth. You are My chosen people and that makes you different. You must then act differently from all other people. You are to be holy to me because I, the Lord, am holy, and I have set you apart from the nations to be my own.[202]

Lord, You certainly have provided us commands and rules about what we do and don't do which we have never heard before.

When you were in Egypt, you had identity as offspring of Abraham but there was little about you that distinguished you from all other peoples. That is no longer the case. You must not do as they do in Egypt, where you used to live, and you must not do as they do in the land of Canaan, where I am bringing you. Do not follow their practices. You must obey my laws and be careful to follow my decrees. I am the Lord your God.[203] Everything you do and think about now characterizes your relationship with Me.

I can see how the holidays and celebrations bring us together as a people in worshipping and honoring You. We share this common faith and encourage each other to keep this relationship with You as Your people. We can celebrate that which makes us different because we know that along with the commands comes Your promises. As Your chosen people, we are different and we thank You for that.

If you consider for example, the Passover, this is a day you are to commemorate; for the generations to come you shall celebrate it as a festival to the Lord—a lasting ordinance.[204] The Israelites are to keep vigil to honor the Lord for the generations to come.[205] I know that this is very personal to you and this generation because you actually experienced the Passover event. But establishing it as a holiday for generations to come, your descendants will share with you in this reality. You must teach your offspring all I have commanded concerning these events. All Israelites and those adopted into the chosen people have this event as part of their heritage and can celebrate My power through the miracles with which I delivered you from Egypt.

I can see also why You instituted priests to work before You. Your tabernacle is also Your dwelling place. It is not open for anyone to intercede with us before You. You rightly insist that those serving directly before You must be properly prepared and rightly respect You for who You are.

I did direct you to have Aaron, your brother brought to you from among the Israelites, along with his sons…so they may serve me as priests.[206] I have given you instructions for how the priests are to represent me to the people and how they relate to the priests. I have given you instructions for the tabernacle. This is all related to My relationship to the whole people. Things you do together help you all maintain your identity as My people as something you all share.

I see the importance of us having a community for worship and offerings. It helps us all to keep a sense of our shared identity. We can support and encourage each other in the faith and through the times that we may not see you so active in our lives. As individuals, we certainly are not allowed to look, dress, or act like anyone else.

For individuals, I have given instructions on what you can and cannot eat, what you can wear, how you groom and adorn yourselves, to keep the Sabbath, that which is clean and unclean and other instructions. You must distinguish between the unclean and the clean, between living creatures that may be eaten and those that may not be eaten.[207] I have set you apart from the nations to be My own. Not only do these commands relate to you as a people, they cause you to think of Me every time you wake, eat, dress, work, relate to your neighbor and all other aspects of life. You used to do whatever you wanted. Now you must think about what it is that I want and that makes you think of Me. These are not arbitrary rules because I want to be difficult. These are to keep you in relationship with Me. These are not snares or traps to catch you doing wrong but keep you doing what is holy and right because that is who I am and it is the best way for you.

Some will see these simply as rules and ritual but I do see that You intend these to be thoughtful and deliberate times of thinking about You and worshipping You as we go about our daily lives. If everything we do is focused on You, we can live in a right relationship with You and each other. But, Lord, you know that we cannot keep from sinning. We are stiff-necked and difficult.

You are correct, the effect of that transgression is separation from me, and separation from others affected. You recall that when Adam and Eve transgressed and they heard me walking in the garden, they hid from [Me] among the trees of the garden.[208] Sin breaks relationships with me and with each other. These relationships must be restored. If any member of the community sins unintentionally and does what is forbidden in any of the Lord's commands, when they realize their guilt and the sin they have committed becomes known, they must bring as their offering for the sin they committed…In this way the priest will make atonement for them for the sin they have committed, and they will be forgiven.[209] I have provided this as a means to retain the relationship I desire and that which is good for you. Sin is not a private matter only between the individual and me but affects the whole community. That is why this is a public offering. Not only is the individual's relationship restored with me but it is restored with the community as well.

We also do not always treat each other as You have commanded.

These relations must also be restored. If anyone sins and is unfaithful to the Lord by deceiving a neighbor about something entrusted to them or left in their care or about something stolen, or if they cheat their neighbor or if the find lost property and lie about it, or if they swear falsely about any such sin that people may commit—when they sin in any of these ways and realize their guilt, they must return what they have stolen or taken by extortion, or what was entrusted to them, or the lost property they found, or whatever it was they swore falsely about. They must make restitution in full, add a fifth to the value to it and give it all to the owner on the day they present their guilt offering...and they will be forgiven for any of the things they did that made them guilty.[210] Here again, this sin is not a private matter between the two but is also a sin against Me and affects the whole community. Restoration is a public event. Restitution is important in restoring that relationship.

You show your love and concern by providing these ways to restore broken relationships. You have also provided other offering opportunities for us to express our love and devotion to you.

Any person can present a burnt offering to Me that displays his devotion in a personal way. The animal is to be a male without defect and thus, shows he places high value on the sacrifice. It is a burnt offering, a food offering, an aroma pleasing to [Me].[211] I recognize the value of the sacrifice and it pleases me that I am honored in this way.

In gratitude for their harvest, people may offer a grain offering of first fruits to Me. They present it to the priest, who shall take it to the altar...as a food offering, an aroma pleasing to [Me].[212]

People may also present a fellowship offering. The fat and internal organs are a food offering, a pleasing aroma. All the fat is [Mine].[213] The rest of the food is shared between the person and the priests.

These offerings are provided to keep our relationships personal and direct. I accept these offerings as pleasing to Me and enjoy the motivation that brings these to the Priest to offer to me. I desire that people draw near to [Me] with a sincere heart and with the full assurance that faith brings, having our hearts sprinkled to cleanse us from a guilty conscience and having our bodies washed with pure water.[214] We still have not talked about the atonement offering but let's discuss that separately in more detail later.

Sexuality

Society at large is changing its collective view on sexuality. Much has changed over the last fifty years even in how this topic is addressed. Many are being challenged with how to deal with gender questions and personal relations. Some will isolate specific areas of sexual behavior from others but is there a foundational view of what should or should not be acceptable?

I would suspect that Moses had the same questions then as we have today and perhaps the conversation went like this.

Moses: Lord, as You have directed me, I'm writing about our past history. I'm confused over events in our past and the commands you have given us in sexual relations. For example, Abraham twice offered his wife to his host at the time saying she was his sister.[215] That is adultery by your commands. After rushing out of Sodom, both of Lot's daughters became pregnant by their father and the descendants of their sons became the nations of Moabites and Ammonites. That was incest.

Okay, Moses. Let's talk about sex. You realize that those events occurred before I provided My commands. Nevertheless, even without the law, they knew that the actions were not what I intended in relationships.

But let's go back to the beginning. I created man but said, "It is not good for the man to be alone. I will make a helper suitable for him"[216] and I made a woman and brought her to Adam. That is my design, that a man leaves his father and mother and is united to his wife, and they become one flesh.[217] This is important here. They become one! They can no longer be separated but everything that one does affects the other. Their families are also thus united so there is one larger family. Living together and keeping my commands together then provides the highest quality of life for them both and is my design. Together they honor and respect me and together they honor and respect their family and neighbors. What I have joined together let no one separate.[218] I desire that you should rejoice in the wife of your youth.[219] The intimate contact between husband and wife is a unique blessing that is reserved for those who are one. As you grow older as one, you grow together and although you don't lose your individual identity, your oneness is strengthened.

Sure, you will have friends of the same sex. Times you will share that can be very personal and fulfilling but when it comes to intimate sexual relations, I had no other design for suitable partners for man or woman. From your beginning when I knit [you] together in [your] mother's womb,[220] your sexual identity was established. I have no other plan. Surely, as I have planned, so it will be, and as I have purposed, so it will happen.[221] While some may be confused about their identity, I am not confused. I am not arbitrary. I don't deceive. When I tell you that you shall not give false testimony,[222] I do not give false testimony. I do not create false testimony.

But I know of people who have been drawn sexually to members of the same sex before You gave us Your command.

You also had people who engaged in sexual relationships with other people's wives or husbands. You had people engaged in prostitution. But you are not to be like other people any longer. Anything that interferes with this union between a man and woman is outside my plan. Any other intimate sexual contact works to destroy this bond. You must not do as they do in Egypt, where you used to live, and you must not do as they do in the land of Canaan, where I am bring you. Do not follow their practices.[223] You are to be holy as I am holy. This include adultery, incest, sex with close relatives on either side, sex with animals, sacrificing children to false gods, prostitution, homosexual relations or any other act or intent that works against this union. Flee from sexual immorality. All other sins a person commits are outside the body, but whoever sins sexually, sins against their own body.[224] And since you are one with your wife or husband or the wife or husband to be, your sin against your own body is a sin against the oneness of the union.

Moses, you singled out two examples but take this plan as a whole for sexual purity. Any sexual contact outside marriage of a man and a woman is against my plan and is hurtful to someone. Ultimately, nothing is private when it goes against this union. I gave you the gift of sexual desire but also am providing the framework under which you should act. I know that people want to make their own choices but that is to put themselves above Me and is idolatry. We talked about that before.

But, Lord, You Yourself said that You gave us the gift of sex. Did You have to make it so important to us?

I give many gifts and have promised you many blessings if you keep My commands. None of these gifts is more important than I. You may be envious of the wealth of others but that envy is against My command. Put Me first in all you do and seek to support each other. Love the Lord your God with all your heart and with all your soul and with all your mind and with all your strength…Love your neighbor as yourself.[225]

You remember when Eve saw that the fruit of the tree was good for food and pleasing to the eye, and also desirable for gaining wisdom, she took some and ate it.[226] She placed her desires above My commands. I know this is not easy and there are many temptations in this world. But in any temptation know this, I will not let you be tempted beyond what you can bear. But when you are tempted, [I] will also provide a way out so that you can endure it.[227]

The world has many enticements for you but it is my plan that sexual relations is an intimate relationship that is reserved. Yes, I designed it to be pleasurable. And it is private. Obviously, it produces offspring and as I told Noah, Be fruitful and increase in number and fill the earth.[228] This family relationship of father, mother and child is my model for the building of community. Add together the extended families of both parents and the collection of friends and their families and you have a community group that can care for the needs of their community. They can care for the widow or the fatherless or the sick or poor. They can lean on each other and hold each other accountable in keeping My commands.

You know that relationships between husbands and wives are not always the best. Even on my way to Egypt, I had a falling out with Zipporah.

Yes, and it saddens Me whenever there is discord in the family. I am love and all my commands relate to how you are to love me and love each other. I'm not talking about sexual desire here or lust but real love. In all your relationships and especially that with husband or wife, love is patient, love is kind. It does not envy, it does not boast, it is not proud. It does not dishonor others, it is not self-seeking, it is not easily angered, it keeps no record of wrongs. Love does not delight in evil but rejoices with the truth. It always protects, always trusts, always hopes, always perseveres. Love never fails.[229]

We don't seem to be made this way because these characteristics are not part of our natural self.

True, but I'm commanding you to be better than your natural self. Be holy, because I am holy.[230] Do nothing out of selfish ambition or vain conceit. Rather, in humility value others above yourselves, not looking to your own interests but each of you to the interests of the others.[231] Imagine both the husband and wife taking this to heart: each seeking to satisfy the interests of the other and holding that interest above their own. Intimate contact then becomes mutually agreeable and satisfying rather than one demanding his or her rights.

What about divorce? We do permit a man to write a certificate of divorce and separate from his wife.

It [is] because your hearts [are] hard.[232] Anyone who divorces his wife and marries another woman commits adultery against her. And if she divorces her husband and marries another man, she commits adultery.[233]

Moses, as we have said, these people are stiff-necked. Some will try to find loopholes in this or other areas of My commands and think that because I may not have explicitly addressed some situation, it is not covered. However, we have covered the context for sexual contact.

Look, Moses. I never said it would be easy to keep My commands. I just command you to do so. You and your people will fail at this. I know this. Don't look upon any one of these areas as being more important than any other. A sin is a sin. But in my love for you, I will provide you a way to atone for your sins and restore the right relationship with Me.

Atonement

How can I get right with God? Can God forgive me for what I've done? What can I do to make up for the mistakes of the past? Have I been that bad that I need a way to get right with God?

This is so important that I'm certain that Moses spoke with God about it. Let's listen in.

Moses: Lord, your commands are hard for us to keep. You have said, "Be perfect, therefore, as [I am] perfect,"[234] but how can we be perfect?

I showed you perfection in the Ten Commandments and the Law. Keep these commands. You are no longer your own. You are My people so be holy, because I am holy.[235]

With our free will, how can we perfectly keep your command? There are too many distractions and we are weak-willed. We will make mistakes. We will sin against you.

Moses, you are correct. For all have sinned and fall short of the glory of God.[236] There is no one righteous, not even one.[237]

But some do seem to lead very good lives. They treat others with respect and dignity. They don't kill or commit adultery. They are honest and appear to have integrity. They support those who are less fortunate.

You are neglecting the first commandments—Love the Lord your God with all your heart and will all your soul and with all your mind.[238] Do they put Me above all else? If they did, they would see where they fall short.

So You require us to be holy, to be perfect but You know that we cannot be. So what can we do?

First, Moses, you need to understand that every time My command is broken, two sins are committed: a sin against Me because it is My law that is broken and a sin against another person and/or a sin against the whole of My chosen people. An individual's sin affects My relationship with all the Israelites. I led you to the land of Canaan and told you to take it but ten of the twelve who went to spy the land rebelled against Me. All the Israelites will suffer as a result of their sin.

Isn't that a bit severe? Millions of us will be affected by the sins of a few.

Those ten were not the only ones who doubted My ability to lead you in victory. But even so, when I say you are My chosen people, I mean all of you. I don't just mean a few here and there. My intent is that all will share in the inheritance in the new land. I promised this to Abraham, Isaac and Jacob and now to you.

Out of all the peoples, I have chosen the Israelites. It is a twoway relationship. I've promised you many blessings as My people but all of you have also promised to obey Me. I know some have difficulty in understanding that I truly want a relationship with each of you and with the whole community.

We do know that when we sin against You, we are breaking that relationship. What can we do to restore it?

That is why I have provided you with instructions for your worship and offerings of sacrifice. Repent, then, and turn to [Me] so that your sins may be wiped out.[239] You can be forgiven and redeemed through the sacrifices I've instituted.

We talked about these sacrifices. There are sacrifices You instituted as a means for us to demonstrate how important You are to us. It's not just about restoring relationships but also in living in the relationship. The fellowship offering is a way for us to show you our continuing devotion to you. The first fruits offering and grain offerings are our way to say thanks. We can privately acknowledge our love for You but this shows the entire community our desire for this relationship with You.

I do enjoy these offerings, they are an aroma pleasing to [Me].[240] The "aroma" includes the whole experience of the offering.

You have also given us instructions for when we sin knowingly or realize it later that we have sinned. These too are public offerings for our guilt and to show repentance but there is one in particular that is of high importance. You have instructed us to set aside one day annually specifically for atonement for our sins.

For those sins that are not recognized or for sin involving all Israel, this atonement day is a special day where all sin is absolved and My relationship with all people is restored. The High Priest shall make atonement for himself and his household and shall bring two goats and present them before Me at the entrance to the tent of meeting. He is to cast lots for the two goats—one lot for the Lord and the other for the scapegoat.[241] He is to sacrifice for a sin offering the goat whose lot falls to the Lord. Then, he shall bring forward the live goat. He is to lay both hands on the head of the live goat and confess over it all the wickedness and rebellion of the Israelites—all their sins—and put them on the goat's head. He shall send the goat away into the wilderness in the care of someone appointed for the task. The goat will carry on itself all their sins to a remote place; and the man shall release it in the wilderness.[242] These innocent animals are taking on your sins and taking the punishment you deserve. The law requires that nearly everything be cleansed with blood, and without the shedding of blood there is no forgiveness.[243]

I understand what You say about the shedding of blood but is there a different way? I mean, these animals are very valuable to us and it is hard for us to see any of your creatures be slaughtered, especially those as innocent and without blemish as these animals we are to sacrifice. Because of our failings, there will be a lot of animals sacrificed each year.

Yes, they are of value to you and that is why you must recognize the gravity of failing to obey me. Before long, you and I will again talk of this and I will tell you of greater things to come. For now, this is your atonement. While you cannot purify yourselves, I have provided you the way. I am the Lord their God.[244]

This is indeed a special day. On this day, the whole nation is restored in our relation with you.

Moses, I want so much to bless all the people. You know that if you follow my decrees and are careful to obey my commands, I will[245] do so many things favorable for you. You will prosper and enjoy peace in the land. I will walk among you and be your God, and you will be my people.[246]

We know you are with us now. This is the way we want our relationship. We love and trust you. Thank you for providing the way for us to keep this relationship.

That is it exactly, Moses. I want to maintain this relationship. But I don't want the people to get the idea that they can do anything they want; knowing that once a year all is forgiven. This is not a ritual for you to do mindlessly and expect that all is well. That is no relationship. I take no pleasure in ritual alone. There is no pleasing aroma in a sacrifice that does not carry the worship or contrition of the offeror.

You must know, Moses, that this is a two-way covenant. The Israelites have committed to following My decrees and commands. But I also warned you of the consequences if you will not listen to me and carry out all these commands, and if you reject my decrees and abhor my laws and fail to carry out all my commands and so violate my covenant,[247] life will become harder for you. I will do this to discipline you to change your ways to come back to Me. The time is coming when these people come near to me with their mouth and honor me with their lips, but their hearts are far from me. Their worship of me [will be] based on merely human rules they have been taught.[248] Continued disobedience will result in increasing difficulty in the discipline I provide. I don't do this because I am vengeful or angry. Yes, it will anger Me but the discipline is to show you your error and that you need to correct it. [My] eyes are too pure to look on evil[249] so to maintain our relationship, you need to be holy. You cannot do this on your own. I will guide you and if you do return to me with your whole heart, I will forgive.

THE WANDERING IN THE DESERT

Numbers 15:1 - 27:11

The Israelites wandered in the desert forty years until the last of the men who were of fighting age (except Caleb and Joshua) died because of their rebellion at Kadesh Barnea. The remaining chapters in Numbers record this time between this rebellion and their final preparations for entering the promised land.

The events of these forty years in the desert are not fully documented in the Bible. However, it was during this time that the Israelites changed from a nation of slaves to a nation of God. The discipline and Law provided by God as well as His direct actions to their times of disobedience solidified His role as their God. This type of "boot camp" was necessary to transform their minds and to train in battle in preparation for the conquest of Canaan.

As the Israelites are being led in the final stages toward their promised land, they wanted to pass through the land of Edom. Edom refused and rather than engage in battle, the Israelites found another route.

The first recorded battle leading up to the entry into the promised land was with the Canaanite king of Arad who lived in the Negev. He attacked the Israelites and captured some. Rather than just retaliate, the Israelites sought God's direction and help. The Lord listened to Israel's pleas and gave the Canaanites over to them.[1] The Israelites completely destroyed these Canaanites as God had commanded them to do.

They then came to the land of the Amorites. Their request to pass peacefully through that land was met with the full force of the Amorite army. The battle ensued and the Israelites prevailed and took over their land.

As the Israelites continued, they encountered the king of Bashan. The Lord said to Moses, "I have delivered him into your hands, along with his whole army and his land."[2] The Israelites took possession of his land.

The Israelites then completed their journey to the edge of the promised land by camping in the land they had taken from the Amorites along the eastern side of the Jordan River across from Jericho.

Moab, the neighboring country south of them, was fearful of the Israelites and conspired with Midian to attack and defeat them. They first sought the assistance of Balaam, who was known to have a special relationship with God to put a curse on the Israelites. Balaam did the opposite in response to directions from God. The activities of Balaam are recorded in Numbers 22:5–24:24.

Midian and Moab then were involved in encouraging many of the Israelites in idol worship of their gods. Some Israelites were persuaded and were punished but here God denounced both Moab and Midian as enemies of Israel. Recall that this is the same Midian to which Moses fled some eighty years before. God directs Moses to send an army against the Midianites and they are victorious.

The Israelites fight additional battles on the eastern side of the Jordan that become a part of the final Israeli boundaries. They are then poised to move against the inhabitants of the promised land.

There were several times in this period when the Israelites grumbled and complained about the leadership of Moses but God reaffirmed Moses as His choice. At one point, Korah led a rebellion against Moses and God punished the rebellious people when the ground opened up and swallowed the leaders and others perished by fire. Still people grumbled against Moses and each time God punished their insolence.

The complaining wore on Moses and although each time he brought the situation to God, his anger at this was displayed at Meribah Kadesh. Recall that all their travels were directed by God's presence and here, there was a shortage of water. They should have known that if God led them to this location, He would provide the water they needed. But again, they compared this current situation back to the plenty they said they had in Egypt.

This time, the grumbling against Moses seems to have gotten under his skin and he reacts in apparent anger. As before, he and Aaron first go to God and fell facedown looking for assistance. While God directs Moses to speak to the rock and it will pour out water, instead he struck the rock twice with his staff and said, "Listen, you rebels, must we bring you water out of this rock?"[3]

Not only does Moses fail to "speak" to the rock but he is taking credit for delivering the water through his own actions. He is rebuked by God: "Because you did not trust in me enough to honor me as holy in the sight of the Israelites, you will not bring this community into the land I give them."[4]

Moses appeals this sentence several times, as we will note later.

During this time of wandering, Moses continued to meet face-to-face with God. God continued to provide directions for the Israelites after conquering the land. While Moses records the death of both Aaron and Miriam, his sister, he does not record the death of his wife. Aaron was 123 years old when he died and Zipporah would likely have been more than one hundred years old. It is possible that she did survive him or that Moses may have thought this too personal to include in his book.

Just prior to moving to the final position to start the attack on Canaan, God directed another count of the men twenty years old or more. The total number of men at this time was 601,730.[5] At the end of the wandering, Moses was 120 years old but the oldest men in the tribes, other than Caleb and Joshua, would be at most sixty years old.

It's about Time

When we look at the timeline for Moses, he was forty years old when he fled to Midian, eighty years old when he returned to lead the Israelites out of Egypt and 120 years old when they arrive near the Jordon. We are impatient people and wonder why God would take so much time to accomplish His plans. Perhaps this conversation can help us understand.

Moses: Oh, Lord, why did you have me wait *forty years* tending sheep before calling me for this task? I was ready in Egypt at age forty but you rebuked me then. When you did call me, I was over eighty years old. I could have been able to accomplish more with You if we started sooner.

Moses, I choose the appointed time[6] but you really have two questions here. What is the nature of "time" and what are the reasons for the apparent delays in your life? First, let's talk about time in general.

We certainly have time for this discussion since we are to remain in the desert until all but Caleb and Joshua die.

Very funny, Moses.

Time is mine. I created it. Time is as I choose and time can be very complex. Future generations will study time to try to understand it but for you, time is constant as a flowing river.

Moses, you sat by the Nile frequently considering the important things in your life. You watched leaves and branches drift along with the current. For you, you are like the branch that floats along and the events in your life are along the shore. You watch or participate in these events but once accomplished, they drift into the past (upstream) and you are not able to return to them. You look downstream at the events that you see coming. You may not see them all and some are surprises. Some you may plan for and in some cases, your decisions may change the way your river flows. However, you cannot see around the upcoming bend in the river. Sometimes you may think you know what lies around that bend but it may not be as you imagine.

You certainly didn't show me what was around the bends for me when you called me at the burning bush.

It is not for you to know what lies ahead but to be obedient to Me. If you had seen all that was in store for you, you may have gone weary and lost heart. Those who hope in [Me] will renew their strength. They will soar on wings like eagles; they will run and not grow weary, they will walk and not be faint.[7] I want and you need to trust and rely on Me and lean not on your own understanding; in all your ways submit to [Me], and [I] will make your paths straight.[8]

Am I not supposed to think ahead and make any plans for the future?

Of course you are. But it would be best for you to include Me in these plans. Consider what I might desire for you and what I might desire you to do. For I know the plans I have for you. Plans to prosper you and not to harm you, plans to give you hope and a future.[9] With Me, the plans of the righteous are just,[10] and I will support and encourage them.

Now, let's get back to the river illustration. Just as each man or woman has his or her river, all the birds and animals and the heavens themselves have rivers of time. I am not like you in My relation with time. I am before time, as you count it, started. I can see all rivers of time. I can go upstream and downstream in each river or all rivers. I can stop your river or all rivers. I can be with you in your river and with Abraham in his river at the same time. I can be in Pharaoh's court with you while walking in the garden with Adam and Eve and answering prayers of people in generations to come. There are events and individuals that I have planned and which [I] will bring about in [my] own time.[11] All rivers, all lives, are important to me and I watch closely. In some rivers, such as yours, I may change the future bends as I wish to accomplish My will, especially for those who love and fear Me and I call to my service. I may change your river as you may ask Me. It is My choice.

Not one [sparrow] will fall to the ground outside [My] care.[12] I watch when the doe bears her fawn.[13] Everything under heaven belongs to me.[14] I laugh at the antics of the baby monkey. I rejoice in my people's faithfulness. I enjoy my creation but not all the actions of the people.

Are you saying that nothing happens to us that is outside Your plan?

No, I am not saying that. You know that it is My plan that all would keep My commands. But I have provided mankind with free will. You do have the option of ignoring the signs and changes I provide and thus ignore Me. Your rivers may flow in ways I don't desire because of the things you have done.

But forty years? Couldn't we have started this sooner?

Moses, I see all rivers. Yours is not the only one. I see the Pharaoh's river, that of the Canaanites, Jethro's, and that of My people. I can change the rivers but each needs to flow as I design. I choose the time for events. Then I orchestrate the rivers to accomplish this. Besides, you were quite headstrong in that murder in Egypt. You needed time to find humility to be ready for obedience.

I suppose the same answer applies to my people. They were in Egypt four hundred years.

Yes, but not all that time was burdensome for them. You also needed this time to multiply into a great nation. Many of you thought I had neglected you for the four hundred years, but when the set time had fully come,[15] I acted. The river for the people needed to flow to prepare them for this time. At the same time, the sin of the Amorites [had] not yet reached its full measure.[16] But you bring up another point about time.

The flow of time is different for you than for me. Since I can stop your river and all rivers or go upstream or downstream, the flow of the river is at My choosing. You cannot change the flow of your river nor that of any river. It passes hour by hour, day by day and year by year. With [Me] a day is like a thousand years, and a thousand years are like a day.[17] I am timeless. That is, I existed before you started measuring time and I will exist long after you are gone from this earth. Eternity is a long time from your point of view.

Well then, please speed up this river we're on so we can get out of this desert.

But seriously, what can You tell me about my future? I know that it ends before You lead this people into the promised land although I'd like to ask you again to change that.

Moses, Caleb and Joshua and the other ten saw this land I promised to Abraham, Isaac and Jacob. It is indeed a beautiful land and is well prepared for My people. When My people are ready to enter and take it from the Canaanites, I'll show it to you but you will not enter it. You will see what I have prepared for them. This is but a glimpse at what you will see when I take you to be with me. What no eye has seen, what no ear has heard and what no human mind has conceived: the things [I have] prepared for those who love [Me].[18] You will enter my rest and be joined to your fathers with me.

Okay, I think I understand that all the events, or rivers, were not ready when I was forty years old to begin this trek through the desert to Midian. But couldn't you have revealed Yourself to me while I was still in Egypt, in Pharaoh's court?

Moses, you were not ready then. You were head strong and arrogant. Basically, you were stiff-necked like the rest of the Israelites. You were in Pharaoh's house and in the line of succession to perhaps be Pharaoh yourself. You would have been considered a god to the Egyptians. You were very well educated and had military training. Nothing seemed impossible to you, even to consider leading a rebellion against Pharaoh. You didn't need me when you decided to try to lead My people. How can you lead My people when you cannot be obedient or dependent upon me? I chose you from your birth for this role. Blessed are those [I] choose and bring near to live in [My] courts![19] I formed your river to be as I need to accomplish My purpose and My promise. You also needed reforming into one who would be willing to follow My direction and be obedient.

Okay, so now I'm forty years old and living in Midian. Why did I have to stay there tending sheep for Jethro for another forty years? Couldn't we have had our meeting and time together; say after ten years or fifteen? Did You really need forty more years?

Moses, I'm in no hurry to accomplish what I want. I do not forget My promises. I am not slow in keeping [My] promise, as some understand slowness.[20] I knew you well before you knew Me. You like action. The situation was not ready and you were not ready to go into action. But when it comes to action, I am the Lord; in its time I will do this swiftly.[21] There was no delay from the time I called you until you went into action.

So you know the end of my time. And You have also revealed that to me. I know I will die before the Israelites are allowed to enter the land you promised. But you have also promised that I will see that land. That means that I will be about 120 years old when I die.

Moses, I know where you are heading with this but let's save that for another time. I also want you to know that time does factor into my relationships. I am patient with you, not wanting anyone to perish, but everyone to come to repentance.[22] I do not rush anyone into a relationship with Me. However, time is short for humankind to repent. Each of you expects to live a long life and each thinks they have plenty of time to consider this. However, as Isaac said, I...don't know the day of my death.[23] Therefore, repent and live.[24]

How Can We Know Your Will

In the ancient world, man-conceived religions involved capricious gods who may have had human-like characteristics. Often, people were totally confused on what they could or should do to please their god and thus, avoid punishment and retribution. While most of these religions are a thing of the past, some today continue to ask what they can do to please God. How can we know if we are doing what He wants or desires? Is there anything we can do that would please Him? How can we know the right direction to take? Perhaps we can learn from Moses's discussion with God.

Moses: Lord, when I was in Egypt, I felt that I was intended to lead the Israelites out of their bondage. Yet, I was totally crushed. Then forty years later, this is exactly what You wanted me to do? I was confused. How can we know what Your will is?

If you know Me, you know My will.

I think I need a bit more clarity.

Your first question was who I am. That is the beginning of knowing Me. You know I am the Creator and I created you out of love. I love you and desire you may have life, and have it to the full.[25] *You also know that I demand that you recognize My place and that I am just and am jealous of My position.*

You have included this in the first commandments.

Yes. In summary, the commandments are to love the Lord your God with all your heart and with all your soul and with all your mind and with all your strength…[and to] love your neighbor as yourself.[26]

You are saying that your commandments then show us Your will?

Yes. If you know My commands and live by them, you are doing My will. This is the basics of a righteous life. This is how I want you to live. It shows you the relationship I want you to have with Me and with each other.

If you have a question whether something is in line with My will or not, check it against My commands. If you are tempted in an affair with another's wife, you know that such actions are against My will. There is no question. If you want to cheat another or gossip, you know that such actions are against My will. The commandments tell you not only what you are to avoid but what you are to do as well. If you are seeking an advantage over another, you are not in My will but if you are supporting and helping another, you are acting in accordance with My will.

We have written down your commands and have talked about them.

That is not enough. These commandments that I give you… are to be on your hearts. Impress them on your children. Talk about them when you sit at home and when you walk along the road, when you lie down and when you get up. Tie them as symbols on your hands and bind them on your foreheads. Write them on the doorframes of your houses and on your gates.[27] *The point is that you are to know them so well and talk of them so often that they become integrated into your life. If you do this, you will not* need to ask if your actions are in accordance with My will. You will know beforehand. Then if you sin, you will know it immediately.

I see now that my action in Egypt was not in accordance with Your will. I killed the Egyptian which was against Your command. I assumed that I knew the right action and did not seek You first.

Yes, first of all, life is My gift and My treasure. It belongs to Me and you have no right to take it without My approval. But in what you did, you were trying to take action without me and that did not honor My place. You cannot be acting in My will when you are actively sinning against Me, even if you are trying to do the right thing.

I think I need a bit of clarification on this. Do you mean that our actions will fail if we are sinning even if we are trying to help others, as you may desire? I mean, I know you desire us not to oppress the widow or the fatherless, the foreigner or the poor.[28] Suppose we are trying to help the orphan or widow. I know these are important to you.

Moses, I will accomplish My will. Surely, as I have planned, so it will be, and as I have purposed, so it will happen.[29] You know that the brothers of Joseph were not acting in love toward him when they sold him into slavery in Egypt. They were acting outside my will. Yet, as Joseph said later to his brothers, "do not be distressed and do not be angry with yourselves for selling me here, because it was to save lives that God sent me ahead of you…God sent me ahead of you to preserve for you a remnant on earth and to save your lives by a great deliverance."[30] I would have accomplished the preservation of this remnant had they not sold Joseph. In addition, these brothers were in agony over what they had done. Now, these brothers were not acting toward the good but even if someone is sinning in trying to do good things, I may use the results to further My will, but the person is still acting outside My will. If the person does not repent, I may remove him or her from that position and give it to another.

Surely, these commands do not cover every situation in which we find ourselves.

Let's think about this. If you lived in accordance with these commands, you will be affirming My place and your relationships with others will be strong. But consider a person's relationship with parents. While the child grows through adolescence and into adulthood, the father and mother's desires are well known by their children. In most circumstances, the child will know what will gain the approval and the disapproval of the parents even if it was not explicitly discussed before. The same is true in your relationship with Me. The more time a person spends in My presence, the more the person is likely to understand My will and do it.

For me it is easy since we talk often. What do the rest of the people do to be in Your presence?

Spend time with Me. As I just said, meditate on My words and commands. Talk of them often. Participate in the festivals and sacrifices I've directed. Spend time with those whose faith is strong. Ask Me to strengthen your faith. We've discussed before the means of increasing faith. Do not forget My teaching, but keep My commands in your heart, for they will prolong your life many years and bring you peace and prosperity. Let love and faithfulness never leave you; bind them around your neck, write them on the tablet of your heart. Then you will win favor and a good name in [My] sight and man. Trust in the Lord with all your heart and lean not on your own understanding; in all your ways submit to [Me], and [I] will make your paths straight.[31] All this renews your mind so do not conform to the pattern of this world, but be transformed by the renewing of your mind. Then you will be able to test and approve what [My] will is—[My] good, pleasing and perfect will.[32]

I understand how important Your law and commands are. I will keep emphasizing that with the Israelites.

Yes, but I don't want you to confuse worship of Me for worship of My laws. The relationship with Me is much more important than the actions you take. For I desire mercy, not sacrifice, and acknowledgment of [Me] rather than burnt offerings.[33] Do not be misled by those who will enforce the laws but ignore My love and concern. I don't appreciate mindless ritual. Going through the motions is not honoring me. I'm looking at the attitudes of your heart. Then your sacrifices and burnt offerings are of value to me and a pleasing aroma. Then we have the relationship I desire.

Are you interested in every decision we make? Is every decision a question of being in tune with Your will?

Moses, I love to be involved in every aspect of everyone's lives. Don't consider any decision too minor to inform Me and ask for My guidance. I know what you need before you ask [Me].[34] In all things [I] work for the good of those who love [Me], who have been called according to [My] purpose.[35] You may think I don't have a preference for a particular decision, such as what you may desire to eat for a meal or what crops to plant, but I would rather you lay all requests before Me and thus, honor Me in your life.

Your commands are those involving relationships.

As you walk in My commands and are mindful of them, you will understand areas of your life that are not in conformance with them. As you understand what you are not to do and obey them, you will also see what you are to do. When you understand what love is as it relates to your neighbor, you will see my desire for you in these relationships.

How do we love our neighbor? What is love?

Love is treating others as you would like to be treated or more perfectly, how I would treat them. Sometimes people don't know how they should treat themselves. Love is patient, love is kind. It does not envy, it does not boast, it is not proud. It does not dishonor others, it is not self-seeking, it is not easily angered, it keeps no record of wrongs. Love does not delight in evil but rejoices with the truth. It always protects, always trusts, always hopes, always perseveres. Love never fails.[36] This is how you should evaluate yourself in relationships with others.

This is hard. I stumble on the very first thing—patience. I'm not patient. It is so evident between us how I lost my temper when I struck the rock for water rather than do what you said. How can we change ourselves?

Moses, when you keep these values in the forefront, you will recognize when you fall short. That helps you the next time you are confronted with the same situation. You learned well the lesson on patience. And these are not meant to be sequential in that you try to master one then the next. I'm saying that you need to master all. Less than that is sin that needs repentance and forgiveness. Lean on Me and seek to keep My commands rather than placing your interests first.

So, if we seek to keep our relationship good with you, and seek to love our neighbor, we are in Your will?

Yes, as you truly begin to love your neighbor in this light, I will reveal to you and you will see what I desire you to do. You must learn to devote [yourselves] to doing what is good, in order to provide for urgent needs and not live unproductive lives.[37]

What about an occupation, vocation, or means of making a living? How can we know what you want us to do or what is in accordance with your will toward us?

There are times I may call a person into direct service to Me as you well know. I have directed here that the Levites are specifically chosen to serve Me. So for others, I also distribute gifts and abilities as I see needs. I know you have need for food, clothing, shelter, and other necessities of life. So I distribute gifts to those who farm, raise sheep, build homes, and so forth. The important point here is that when you are doing this work; consider how your actions are in accordance with my will. Whatever you do, work at it with all your heart, as working for the Lord.[38] If you know you are working for me, it will guide you in your relations with others. This too, is My will for you.

Finally, even though the Levites are specifically called to serve Me, some may find some of My people in need and have a desire to help or serve them. Administer true justice; show mercy and compassion to one another. Do not oppress the widow or the fatherless, the foreigner or the poor.[39] This may become clear as they seek to love their neighbor as we discussed. This too, then is in My will.

Obedience

If then we seek God's will and He shows us what He wants us to do, what then do we actually do? This is a very personal question for many of us. For me personally, as I mentioned before, the church, of which I was a member, was in an urgent building mode and it was suggested that we pray for what God would want us to contribute. My wife and I decided to do so independently and both received a response of the same amount that far exceeded our expectations or ability. What do you do with that? Do you ask again thinking you misheard? To whom would you seek a second opinion? I cannot stress enough the blessings that come from obedience.

For those with military, law enforcement or firefighting experience, obedience is obeying the orders of superiors. It is understood that superiors have greater experience or understand the bigger picture so that following orders is ingrained in discipline. In other environments, we may be faced with similar circumstances. What does God say about obedience to Him? Let's listen in to Moses having this discussion.

Moses: As I'm thinking about the beginning, I am focused on Adam and Eve. Their sin was to eat of the fruit of the tree against your explicit instruction. Their sin was one of disobedience. I know You are serious about obedience.

For Adam and Eve, it was really more than disobedience. They believed in their arrogance that they could make their own decisions, even contrary to Me, so it was an act of rebellion. But now, this discussion about obedience will be a short one. You know that My commands display what is required. The people publicly announced, "We will do everything the Lord has said."[40] I expect they will. If not, they are in sin and must seek atonement.

Noah and Abraham are well known for their obedience. It must have been very difficult for both of them. Noah built the ark and brought in the animals when there was no imminent indication of any flood or disaster. He must have endured ridicule from all the people around him. He likely did so anyway because of his righteousness and their corruptness.

By faith Noah, when warned about things not yet seen, in holy fear built an ark to save his family. By his faith he condemned the world and became heir of the righteousness that is in keeping with faith.[41]

Abraham showed full obedience when he left his home to go where You directed him. He had no idea what was ahead for him.

By faith Abraham, when called to go to a place he would later receive as his inheritance, obeyed, and went, even though he did not know where he was going.[42]

Both of them are described as righteous even though You had not yet provided anyone your commands. They had a right relationship with You.

They both recognized Me as their Lord and were obedient to My will. They desired to honor Me and follow My direction for them. When I told Abraham to count the stars—if he could and said, "So shall your offspring be,"[43] Abraham believed Me and I credited it to him as righteousness.[44]

I think a more difficult situation for Abraham came when you called him to sacrifice his son Isaac as an offering to You and he obeyed. When You saw he would obey, You stopped him. He could have obeyed You or obeyed his own heart to save his son and chose correctly.

Don't you know that when you offer yourselves to someone as obedient slaves, you are slaves of the one you obey—whether you are slaves to sin, which leads to death, or to obedience, which leads to righteousness?[45] Some may in their behaviors, such as greed or lust, set themselves up in a slave relationship with that behavior.

We have talked about unintentional or intentional breaking of Your commands and that they require sacrifice and atonement to restore the relationship with you. After atonement, their relationship has been restored but they may still have to deal with the consequence of their sin. Sometimes, people like to justify their own actions by claiming Your commands may not be explicit enough. Or others may have legitimate questions about what You mean by "Remember the Sabbath day by keeping it holy."[46] On the Sabbath, we are not to do any work. We have to understand what is meant by "work."

Moses, My will is for the right relationships with My people and the right relationships between people. If the commands are taken in this understanding, the areas of question will likely disappear. Is someone trying to maintain the right relationship with Me or not? Are they trying to maintain the relationship with others that I desire or not? It is difficult for you to understand the motivation of others, but I see the heart.

I didn't want to lead the people when you told me to. Your directions were very clear but I didn't want to obey and You became angry with me. I didn't know You before that. I certainly didn't know You as I do now.

I understand and took that into account at the time. Yes, I was angered at your reluctance and arguments. However, you did obey Me and did do as I commanded.

I am totally in service to You, Lord. How about the sons of Aaron, Nadab and Abihu? They too were actually in service to You.

They took it upon themselves to make decisions related to My instructions. They acted in My place in trying to set up the worship they thought I wanted.

I think I see that also with respect to my actions at Kadesh. You told me "Speak to that rock before their eyes and it will pour out its water."[47] Rather, in my frustration with the people, I struck the rock twice with my staff.

You also said, "Listen, you rebels, must we bring you water out of this rock?"[48] You were taking credit for My work. You have been forgiven for this action but still will have to endure the consequences.

I see that there are no options for partial obedience to Your word or commands. What You command, You expect to be completed exactly as You direct.

Walk in obedience to all that [I have] commanded you, so that you may live and prosper and prolong your days in the land that you will possess.[49]

You have provided a promise here that we may "live and prosper". However, I know we should not expect reward for obedience. When [we] have done everything [we] were told to do, [we] should say "We are unworthy servants; we have only done our duty."[50] Nevertheless, You continue to shower us with grace.

Conflict and Warfare

In the world today, one may think life is fairly safe and stable with most countries respecting their boundaries and few seeking to take land and plunder from others. However, recent history shows Russia taking the Crimea and other lands from Ukraine, ISIS taking land from Syria and Iraq and not too far back, historically speaking, Germany fighting two world wars seeking to conquer land and Japan initiating a war to preserve access to resources. We are faced with terrorism and gun violence. Ancient times were also scary when individuals or counties sought to conquer surrounding land and peoples. In the ancient world, the Babylonians, the Hittites, the Amorites, the Hyksos, the Egyptians, and many other groups fought for control of the Middle East prior to the time of Moses.

Moses' training would certainly have included military service and strategy. The Egyptians were a mighty force at the time and as a potential future Pharaoh, he would have been well schooled in military tactics and strategy. He may have participated in military battles for the Egyptians prior to his exile. What equipment and strategy was available at his time?

Gunpowder was invented by the Chinese in the ninth century AD and not available until much later than Moses. Weapons of war primarily consisted of swords, spears, battle axes and similar hand held weapons, slings, and bows and arrows. The Egyptians were particularly skilled in using chariots and used them during the Exodus[51]. Swords at the time of Moses were primarily made of bronze.[52] These swords had a maximum length of about three feet. This required very close contact with an opponent. The earliest known composite bow (a bow made from a number of materials) was used by Egyptian warriors on chariots and is believed to have been made by at least 2,800 BCE.[53]

When the Israelites first left Egypt, God did not lead them on the shortest route to the promised land. That road led through the Philistine country. At that point, God said, "If they face war, they might change their minds and return to Egypt."[54] However, shortly after leaving Egypt, the Israelites were attacked by the nomadic tribe of the Amalekites so they did face war early on. However, this band was not of the same fighting caliber as the Philistines. Moses sent Joshua to lead the Israelites in the battle and God granted them the victory. About two years later after spying out the land and hearing God's verdict at their disobedience, some tried to fight the Canaanites and Amalekites against God's direction and they were defeated.

The next recorded battle is about thirty-eight years later leading up to the entry into the promised land with the Canaanite king of Arad in the Negev. Joshua will eventually lead the Israelites in the battles to take the land promised by God and it is assumed that Joshua would have used the thirty-eight years to build a well-trained fighting force. Still, it was the Lord who won the victories for them.

Moses then was well educated in warfare. However, he didn't try to muster up an Israeli army against Pharaoh at the Red Sea. He knew what was coming later and likely had discussions with God about it.

Moses: Lord, I want to talk to you about fighting and warfare. We are about to enter the land You promised Abraham, Isaac, and Jacob and to us. We do know that the peoples living there will not just let us take it so we are likely to face war with them. Wars are so devastating; isn't there another way?

Moses, let's start this discussion with I'm very much opposed to wars and conflicts. In fact, I say blessed are the peacemakers, for they will be called children of God.[55] If it is possible, as far as it depends on you, live at peace with everyone.[56] If everyone would live with My commands in righteousness, there would be peace because all these commands desire you to care for each other and tend to each other's needs.

But we know that not everyone will live by Your commands. Conflicts will arise between peoples that cannot be easily resolved.

Conflict is a result of broken relationships. If people lived by My commands and practiced love toward each other, differences could be worked out before becoming conflict.

But the differences people see in each other are frequently the cause of their conflict.

I created humankind in My image so I created differences in looks, personality, talents, and interests. I created this so you could rely on each other to be complete. You are not complete alone. Some feel threatened or fearful when confronted with differences. Others are able to see My creativity.

But there are some people who just rub me the wrong way. It seems to be mostly personality types.

I didn't say that you had to like everyone. I expect that people will have differing viewpoints or ways of handling situations. But do not let a difference lead to conflict. [I do] not look at the things people look at. People look at the outward appearance, but [I] look at the heart.[57] We defined what love was before. That's the way you should treat others, even if you don't like them or want to be in their company.

Some see differences as a point of distinction that makes them belittle the other or feel superior in some way. That was the case even with Aaron and Miriam derided me because of Zipporah's nationality. You showed them the error of their thoughts and actions but they are leaders. They should have known this to be against Your commands.

I hate arrogance and I hate bullying. Do nothing out of selfish ambition or vain conceit. Rather, in humility value others above yourselves, not looking to your own interests but each of you to the interests of the others.[58] This is not easy for humankind to do. It takes work and deliberate actions to have this mind-set. People are deceived if they think they can elevate themselves by putting others down. A perverse person stirs up conflict, and a gossip separates close friends.[59] This would be negated if they would consider the interests of the others.

I can see some thinking that others may be a threat to them or their way of life. That is how Edom treated us. I know we were a large group but we just wanted to pass through their land. We even offered to pay for any water we used. I'm sure they felt their lives and property were in danger from us.

If they had properly evaluated the situation, they would have known that you had no interest in taking their land. That was not the land I was giving you. They could have become a friendly nation had they supported your plans. They acted rashly but it was best for you to avoid them anyway, for now.

It seems like negative feelings and thoughts based upon a difference like this can grow into negative talk and action that later leads to conflict and bloodshed. That's what happened with Miriam and Aaron about Zipporah. You punished Miriam for her talk but I'm not sure it changed her heart.

Again, I'm not saying that you have to like everyone but just treat everyone with love and respect. That part is a decision you make in accordance with My commands. If Miriam still harbored a dislike for Zipporah, that would have been her issue and not Zipporah's. Pride goes before destruction, a haughty spirit before a fall.[60]

I see conflicts here among the Israelites and we are the same people descended from Abraham, Isaac, and Jacob. Often I have to judge between them.

It is right that they bring their disputes to you. That is the way that conflicts should be handled. If your brother or sister sins, go and point out their fault, just between the two of you. If they listen to you, you have won them over. But if they will not listen, take one or two others along, so that every matter may be established by the testimony of two or three witnesses.[61] This also means that if one comes to another with an issue or grievance, both must listen carefully to see if the complaint has merit. If so, each must be willing to concede that and seek restoration. Sometimes there may not be a clear offender and one offended but disputes may be resolved by compromise. If that is unsuccessful, your people know they can take the matter to the judges of ten, fifties, hundreds, or thousands as you have set up. Finally, if it remains unresolved, they can take the matter to you. In the end, they must abide by the decision of the judges.

In spite of these steps, some may not accept the verdict and retain bad feelings.

All should recognize that the ruling of the judge will settle the matter. If they won't, it doesn't make sense to go through the process. Then, as you say, the conflict remains unresolved. Eventually, the one who feels wronged will attempt to get restoration in some way. You know that an angry person stirs up conflict and a hot-tempered person commits many sins.[62]

I see cases come before me that are the results of real or perceived personal injury when someone did something to another or someone's animals wronged another or someone's possessions caused injury to another.

Moses, you know that many of the commandments deal directly with how people should relate to each other. I specifically direct you to avoid murder, false testimony, stealing, adultery, and envy of another's possessions or family. These are usually the areas from which conflicts arise. But among you there must not be even a hint of sexual immorality, or of any kind of impurity, or of greed, because these are improper for God's holy people.[63] We have already discussed restitution in the case of intentional misconduct. Accidental injury may require adjudication before a judge.

Like Edom, the Egyptians were also threatened by us. They kept us as slaves and mistreated us because we had grown into a large nation and because we were different from them. They felt threatened by us because they perceived we would join others in a war against them. The Israelites had no such intention. In fact, they did not even want to leave Egypt until You directed us. Even then, we did not go to war against them—we simply wanted to leave. So their pursuit of us was to preserve their slave labor.

Moses, the Pharaoh may have been correct in his assessment of the danger because oppressed people frequently do revolt against oppressive leaders. You saw this and would have started a revolt had you been more prepared and had the people supporting you. They weren't ready yet.

Is that type of warfare acceptable to you? Is it okay for people to fight for their freedom?

Okay, now you are getting back to your original question. But let's start with this thought. Generally, Moses, let everyone be subject to the governing authorities, for there is no authority except that which [I have] established. The authorities that exist have been established by [Me]. Consequently, whoever rebels against the authority is rebelling against what [I have] instituted, and those who do so will bring judgment on themselves.[64] But this assumes the one in authority is [My] servant for your good.[65] The Pharaoh was in authority was for the good of the Egyptians but not for the good of the Israelites. Had Pharaoh treated the Israelites as he did the Egyptians, it would have been a different situation.

You have given us commands on how we are to treat our servants and slaves. We are not to oppress them but we are to care for them.

Moses, I know that some see this as a way of fulfilling their personal obligations but I would prefer not to see any slavery, even if that slave is well treated. They are to be treated as workers hired from year to year; you must see to it that those to whom they owe service do not rule over them ruthlessly…they and their children are to be released in the Year of Jubilee.[66] There should be no "master" other than Me.

So if people are being oppressed and the governing authorities are not considering the good of the people, do You find it acceptable for them to revolt?

It would be better as we discussed if they could take their grievances before the governing authorities to seek change. But let's be careful here. Let's look at the motivation for the grievances. Are they based on the relationships that I command or are there other reasons: hate, arrogance, feelings of superiority, greed, or other improper motives?

Do you always help one side against another in a conflict like You did with us with the Amalekites?

The Amalekites attacked you without provocation. They were trying to raid and steal from you. That's the greed I'm talking about. Of course, I would work to protect you. You are My people. But if you are asking if I always pick a side, that's a harder question. I have a plan for this world. If I plan it, it will come to be as we have talked about before. How I accomplish that plan is My work. I may want to use a nation's strength in war to carry out parts of that plan. I may also want to use a nation's strength in war to punish another. In every case, however, I am there with those who are fighting regardless of which side they are on.

How can you be there for both sides?

I may not be there for determining the winner of the conflict, but to be there with each individual as the battle rages. I care about each person, on either side. I take no pleasure in the death of anyone.[67] Some may be there not because they are fighting for a cause but because they are ordered into the fight. In any event, you know that my eye is on each person and I care for them.

This is too wonderful. What is mankind that you are mindful of them, human beings that you care for them?[68] This is something that is hard for many to understand. You are God of the universe, yet you care for each of us individually.

There may be those who love me on both sides as well as those who are indifferent to me on both sides. A victory in battle does not mean that I am with the victor nor that I am against the vanquished.

Lord, You have set us up to be different. We are Your people and are not to be like those around us. People will hate us because we are different.

This is the case. As long as you do follow My commands and show yourself to be different from the world, people will hate you. But if you no longer keep My commands and do as the world does, it will not hate you. If you belonged to the world, it would love you as its own. As it is, you do not belong to the world, but I have chosen you out of the world. That is why the world hates you.[69]

The people in these lands know You are with us. They know of Your works in Egypt. They fear us and hate us because You are with us. We will go into battle against them because You are directing us to do so and because You have promised this land as ours. But what of these people that are already here? Can you find another place for them?

Moses, not only is this land that which I promised you and your ancestors but your war against the people is punishment for their evil ways. We talked of this earlier. The evil deeds of the wicked ensnare them; the cords of their sins hold them fast. For lack of discipline they will die, led astray by their own great folly.[70] They have done such evil in My sight that they now face judgment.

You have told us to put all to the sword, to spare no one. Is there none that should survive?

Do not make a covenant with them or with their gods. Do not let them live in your land or they will cause you to sin against me, because the worship of their gods will certainly be a snare to you.[71]

Might there be some righteous people there, perhaps some who do not partake in this evil?

Moses, this is for Me to judge. We will talk about judgment later but My judgment is true and right. I will judge each person's righteousness. Each will come before Me at the judgment day and I know how to rescue the godly from trials and to hold the unrighteous for punishment on the day of judgment.[72]

Lord, we are obeying You in our battles and in our conquest of this land. There are others who say they are fighting for their god or gods in battle. They believe they are acting in obedience to their god.

But if their god is false, and we know it is since I am alone, some person is making up the motivation for battle. It is not a god or Me that is driving that conflict. A good man brings good things out of the good stored up in him, and an evil man brings evil things out of the evil stored up in him.[73] Check the motivation behind the battle and you will find the evil motives. As we discussed before, it could be based on hatred, greed, fear, lust, or other impure motives. Those are worldly motives. Put to death, therefore, whatever belongs to your earthly nature: sexual immorality, impurity, lust, evil desires, and greed, which is idolatry.[74] Seek Me and My will. You will seek me and find me when you seek me with all your heart.[75]

Lord, when Korah, son of Izhar, and others rebelled against Aaron and me during our wandering in the desert, they said that I had gone too far! The whole community is holy, every one of them and the Lord is with them…and that Aaron and I set ourselves above the Lord's assembly.[76] They said they were doing Your bidding.

You know that was not from Me. They acted on their own for their own self-interest and envy. You acted correctly in bringing that to Me to judge and correct. Dathan and Abiram, the sons of Eliab, even described Egypt as a land flowing with milk and honey.[77] That place where they were enslaved they described in that manner. They were rebelling against Me since I had placed you in leadership.

I know you Lord and I know that if You decided that I was not capable of leading this people, You would correct me or release me and find a replacement. But You would not have me guess your intention. How are we to discern whether someone who claims to be speaking on Your behalf is telling the truth?

I am against the prophets who steal from one another words supposedly from me. Yes…I am against the prophets who wag their own tongue and yet declare, "The Lord declares."[78] I will deal with them but you should listen for the motivation for their message. If it is truly from Me, it will be in accordance with My will. It will be in accordance with My character and be expressed in love, as I am love. If the prophesy is from Me, it will come to pass. By their fruit you will recognize them.[79] By their actions and outcomes, you will know whether it is of Me.

I heard You say it will be expressed in love. What do You mean by that?

I am love. Therefore, actions on My behalf in accordance with My will are expressed in love. You cannot force someone to faith. I want all people to be saved and to come to a knowledge of the truth.[80] But faith cannot be forced. Behavior can be forced but I don't desire obedience simply by forced behavior. I desire correct behavior because of the loving relationship I have with people. My commands are true and good but you won't be able to convince people of that by creating conflict or shouting at them. Express My love in your relationships. You are the light of the world…let your light shine before others, that they may see your good deeds and glorify [Me] in Heaven.[81]

This is hard to do because often our good intentions are met with resistance or indifference.

Even though you may not like someone or they may not like you, you are to treat them with love. This is on you, not on how others act. This is to be part of your character. If you love those who love you, what credit is that to you? Even sinners love those who love them.[82] Love your enemies and pray for those who persecute you.[83]

I understand that the world is in conflict and may always be because You are not accepted as God by all and even those of us who believe in You may not be acting in accordance with Your will. I will exhort Joshua and the other leaders to be obedient to your command in seizing the land.

There is one more thought about peace, Moses. It is true that mortals, born of woman, are of few days and full of trouble.[84] Conflict is a part of this world ever since the fall, the sin of Adam and Eve and will continue to be until the end. Conflict will rise up between family members, neighbors, and countries. But even with that conflict and unsettling circumstances, you can be at peace. This peace is a peace in the heart, soul, and mind that comes from trusting Me and being in the right relationship with Me. There is no peace… for the wicked.[85] But [I] will keep in perfect peace those whose minds are steadfast, because they trust in [Me]. Trust in the Lord forever, for the Lord, the Lord himself is the Rock eternal.[86]

In the Beginning

What was it like at the beginning of time? God says that He existed before time for us began. Did the universe come to be at a Big Bang? Was this Big Bang a result of a previous great collapse? Did God cause this Big Bang to occur? Has everything proceeded through evolution or through intelligent design? Did all this come to be about six thousand years ago with six twenty-four-hour periods? Moses was directed by God to write about the beginning. Are his writings relevant to us today?

Let's first review what Moses may have understood about the universe at his time about 3,500 years ago.

Cosmology and Creation

Related to astronomy, cosmology is the study of the largest-scale structures and dynamics of the universe (i.e. galaxies, galaxy clusters, etc.) and fundamental questions about its origin and evolution. The earliest theories of the universe were developed by the Alexandrian astronomer and mathematician Ptolemy about 150 AD, well after the time of Moses.

> The Ptolemaic system is a geocentric cosmology;
> that is, it starts by assuming that the Earth is stationary
> and at the centre of the universe.[87]

At the time of Moses, the cosmos was simply understood by the observation of the stars and planets. Any understanding of the creation of the universe would have been based upon their religious understanding in which Moses would most likely have been schooled.

> In one Egyptian creation myth, the sun god Ra takes the form of Khepri, the scarab god who was usually credited as the great creative force of the universe. Khepri tells us, "Heaven and earth did not exist. And the things of the earth did not yet exist. I raised them out of Nu, from their stagnant state. I have made things out of that which I have already

made, and they came from my mouth." It seems that Khepri is telling us that in the beginning there is nothing. He made the watery abyss known as Nu, from which he later draws the materials needed for the creation of everything.

He goes on to say, "I found no place to stand. I cast a spell with my own heart to lay a foundation in Maat. I made everything. I was alone. I had not yet breathed the god Shu, and I had not yet spit up the goddess Tefnut. I worked alone." We learn that by the use of magic Khepri creates land with its foundation in Maat (law, order, and stability). We also learn that from this foundation many things came into being. At this point in time Khepri is alone. The sun, which was called the eye of Nu, was hidden by the children of Nu. It was a long time before these two deities, Shu and Tefnut were raised out of the watery chaos of their father, Nu. They brought with them their fathers eye, the sun. Khepri then wept profusely, and from his tears sprang men and women. The gods then made another eye, which probably represents the moon. After this Khepri created plants and herbs, animals, reptiles and crawling things.[88]

Moses: Lord, can we talk about the beginning? Some think that things have always been as they are now. We have the stories that have been passed down for generations but we know we can trace our ancestors to Adam and Eve and no further, so there must have been a beginning. How did all this come to be?

Moses, I created it.

I know, but how?

I spoke and it came to be.

I guess I'm looking for a sequence of events. You have directed me to write these things. How am I to describe it? The Egyptians and others have their stories but I want to hear from you what you did.

Is that really an important topic for you? The more important point is why I created it.

Well, I believe that You did create all things. And I believe that Your understanding of things is well beyond mine.

Moses, do you think all things today are the same as they have always been?

No. I've seen the pyramids. They were built by pharaohs long ago.

Do you think I could have created all things with pyramids already there?

You are certainly capable of creating anything you desire. But I don't think You would have created the world with pyramids there.

And why not?

That would be false evidence. It would give us the impression that something came before, but if You created the pyramids at the time of creation, nothing would have come before. It is not your nature to give false testimony because it is against Your own command. But I've heard the creation stories of others who talk about their gods and they don't make sense.

Moses, it is going to be very important for people in years to come to have a written account of My activities, your ancestors and of all the events you have been going through. I will inspire others in the future to continue to record My story and that will continue to add to the information. These will all be a means to encourage faith so I will talk to you about the beginning. When it is time for you to begin to write about everything from the beginning until now, I'll guide you to make sure that you write an accurate account of what I desire to be included.

Before we start, I will tell you that in the future, people will gain greater knowledge and understanding about how this physical world operates and this will be a huge topic of study many years from now. Even though you are a very well-educated man, there are things beyond your understanding that people in the future will understand. There will be things in fact that humans will never understand. It does make it a bit difficult to tell you the story of creation because it does involve topics of which you have had no education. It means that you will need to rely on faith in Me when you don't understand.

I know that people are curious, just as I was with the burning bush, and will continue to investigate things they see and grow in understanding. I have no issue with others surpassing my knowledge level.

Moses, before time began, I am. You can have no concept of time before I created the heavens and the earth. It doesn't have any meaning for you but I am eternal. For My own reasons, I desired to bring this into existence. So when I say, in the beginning [I] created the heavens and the earth,[89] I mean in the beginning of time as it makes sense for humans to think about and understand.

As the word means, before I created it, nothing existed. There was nothing…no light, no forms, no features, nothing.

Do you mean like the inside of a dark cave?

I mean nothing—not even a cave or a mountain in which the cave would be.

Now, as you have gotten to know Me, you know that I am a God of order. I establish[es] order in the heights of heaven.[90] There is no chaos in what I do and so it was in the beginning. I spoke and at that moment, everything that you see and even that which you can't see came into existence although not in the forms that you see now. In a single instant, that energy was focused into a new space and the heavens came into existence, but again, not as you see it today.

It took quite a bit of time before the heavens were prepared for the earth to be fully formed including time for the sun to come into being.

Do you mean that the sun and the earth were not created as we see them now at that moment? How did the sun come into being?

Moses, that is a topic beyond your understanding. In the future, it will be studied as cosmology. But for now, let it be that the sun was formed first and the earth then was formless and empty. Over a period of time as the earth's form took shape, the first thing that occurred here was when I said let there be light. And there was light.[91] If there had been a person on the earth at that time, they could have recognized the difference between the light and darkness but the sky wasn't clear enough yet to make out any shapes or sources of the light.

Sounds like a cloudy day.

I suppose it would have been a similar effect. As the earth continued, I separated the waters on the earth from those above it so the sky with the atmosphere was made.

I think I can see the progression here. It seems like a jar of dirty water left standing for a time when the dirt slowly settles to the bottom and the water clears above it.

That is quite a simplification but perhaps can do. Then I gathered the waters on the earth together in different places so that dry land would appear. Once that dry land appeared, I could continue with making the land produce vegetation: seed-bearing plants and trees on the land that bear fruit with seed in it.[92] This was especially fun as I could play with many different colors but especially the green of the plants. This form of life needed to come before the others so there would be food for them.

If the plants are food for the birds and animals, where do the plants get their food?

The green parts in the plants allow them to absorb light and they can produce their own food using that and the riches of the soil. The green plants also absorbed some of the gases in the atmosphere that would not support other life and replaced it with gases that would. I was pleased with what had been created to this point.

As I caused the sky and atmosphere to continue to clear, the stars, the sun, and the moon would come into clear focus. These lights in the vault of the sky separated the day from the night. They came to be when I ordered the light but now they were visible to serve as signs to mark sacred times, days, and years. The sun provides the difference between day and night: between light and darkness.

So how was the sun formed? It seems and looks like a hot fire burning in the sky. Like the burning bush, it is not consumed.

Moses, this is one of the topics that is beyond your understanding. This will be called a study in nuclear physics in the future. But it does give light and warmth to the earth.

I always wondered why the sun rises in the east and sets in the west but somehow gets back to the east by the next morning. Can you explain that?

People in the future will figure that one out with planetary science. It's not important for you now.

I wondered about the moon also. It appears to be about the same size as the sun but isn't nearly as bright and changes its shape in a manner that we can track. It also changes its position with respect to the stars every night. Why does it do that?

Moses, there are those who are watching and tracking the heavenly bodies very closely now in the field of astronomy but these things are not essential to understand My creation activities. Let's get back to the earth. Once the waters were gathered together, I desired to let the waters teem with living creatures, and let birds fly above the earth across the vault of the sky.[93] Now, it took some time for all this to take place. As with the dry land, I first made the food for the fish and other life and directed a growth and progression of fish as was right. The birds progressed in a similar manner and they had the seed of the vegetation for food. Again, I was pleased with what I saw.

Lord, I always wondered why there were so many different kinds of fish or birds or animals. You didn't just make one or two different kinds of them.

That was part of the fun of creation. What I imagined, I brought into being. I had a lot of different ideas designing the birds, fish and plants and also the animals that would come next on the land. I formed out of the ground all the wild animals and all the birds in the sky.[94] That was the next period, creating the animals. I created many different kinds and forms because I enjoyed it but also because I knew you would enjoy them. They have different functions and abilities. Some run fast, some are terribly slow. Some are very tall and others are short. Some are big and others tiny. Some have very distinct physical features. I had fun doing this.

Was this when the serpent was made also?

There were snakes on the earth as part of the life developed but the serpent of Satan didn't arrive yet.

So, when this period came to maturity, I enjoyed everything I had made to this point. This was a wonderful environment. I love to see the horse leap like a locust, striking terror with its proud snorting[95]…and the eagle soar and build its nest on high.[96] I watch when the doe bears her fawn.[97] Look at the Behemoth, which I made along with you and which feeds on grass like an ox. What strength it has in its loins, what power in the muscles of its belly![98] The wonders and beauty of the flowers, the natural environments for all creatures were good and wonderful and I enjoyed My creation. I laugh at the antics of the baby animals as they play and learn their way. I wonder at the whales as they leap in the oceans. What joy there is in My creation! It was good.

Why did you make flies? I don't see any purpose for flies except for our annoyance.

There may be purposes for the created things that you cannot see or understand.

We as humans are similar to the animals. Did we come from them?

No. This was a separate and fully different creation. And this gets to the more important question I alluded to earlier. Why did I create the heavens and the earth? I don't care if you understand how it came to be. I do care if you understand why I did so.

Lord, I have been with you for some time now and I know you are a God of love. I'd say you created us to love us and for us to love You.

That was the whole point of the creation. I was not satisfied with the creation I made up to this point. It was good but it had no relationship with me. The animals, fish, and birds could not love Me. I could love them and care for them but there was no real relationship.

Even Your commands start with Your desire for a relationship with us.

Moses, there are relationships here in the spiritual realm but there is a difference. Here I am seen and heard and it takes no faith to know Me. For humans, I designed it so that there would be no proof of My existence so the relationship would be based on faith. This is the difference. You have a relationship with Me because I want it and you want it. Without both of us in this, there is no relationship.

You have said that in the future, people will have a greater understanding of Your creative actions. Will they then find proof that You did this?

No. Faith is confidence in what [you] hope for and assurance about what [you] do not see.[99] If one was faced with absolute proof of My existence and actions, there would be no room for faith. A relationship with Me would then be based upon fear or resignation rather than love.

Were Adam and Eve your first human creations?

When the time was right and the Earth fully prepared, I created mankind in [My] own image…male and female [I] created them.[100] They were Adam and Eve.

So you created them purposefully and directly.

Yes. First, I created the man Adam. I formed a man from the dust of the ground and breathed into his nostrils the breath of life, and the man became a living being.[101] I placed this man in the garden I planted called Eden. Man needs a meaningful purpose in life so I gave him the responsibility to work it and take care of it. I also gave him the responsibility of naming all the living creatures.

So Adam was alone as a human at first.

Yes, but it was not good for the man to be alone. [I decided to] make a helper suitable for him.[102] There were no suitable helpers for the man with the animals or birds.

We know of animals of similar stature to man. Could one of these have been a suitable helper?

No. They have not been created in My image. But it is not good for anyone to be alone. One can be active and work hard but one still needs to have someone to share their life. So I created the woman. I caused Adam to fall into a deep sleep and while he was sleeping, [I] took one of the man's ribs and then closed up the place with flesh.[103] [I] then made a woman from the rib I had taken out of the man.[104]

So then, you created the woman and the man. But this was different. You said that you formed the woman from the man's rib but for the other creatures; you formed them from the ground.

Good point. Yes, this was different from the animals and it is because of the very special relationship I desire for the man and woman. The relationship between a man and a woman is totally different than the relationships between animals. Some would like to treat them as the same and actually act like they see animals act. That is not my design. Man and woman are part of each other and I intend that a man and a woman unite again in marriage so that is why a man leaves his father and mother and is united to his wife, and they become one flesh.[105]

So, man and woman are part of the same creation. They are separated but through marriage, they are again united.

Yes. This relationship is different from all the others in creation. And after I created the man and woman, [I] saw all that [I] had made, and it was very good.[106]

As I stare into the sky at night and when I consider your heavens, the work of your fingers, the moon and the stars, which you have set in place, what is mankind that you are mindful of them, human beings that you care for them?[107] I am in awe of how vast are the heavens and how small we are. You said that You created us in Your image. What do you mean by that?

I created mankind to be fully relatable to Me. You are not Me nor do you have the future to be Me. But you have spirit and soul like Me. You have reasoning powers and are capable of critical thought. You have the ability to understand Me and choose to love and follow or not. You have the capability of love; both of a deep personal nature and a more general way of relating to others. While you are finite in your earthly life, your spirit lives beyond this earthly life. Each of you has specific gifts and talents that relate to Mine. That is, some of you are especially gifted in fashioning things with your hands. Look what I fashioned.

In the building of the tabernacle I knew you had given special abilities. I certainly could not do what Bezalel son of Uri did. You filled him with the Spirit of God, with wisdom, with understanding with knowledge and with all kinds of skills to make artistic designs for work in gold, silver and bronze, to cut and set stones, to work in wood and to engage in all kinds of artistic crafts.[108] The same is true for Oholiab son of Ahisamak, You filled with skill to do all kinds of work as engravers, designers, embroiderers in blue, purple and scarlet yarn and fine linen.[109]

Some of you are gifted in song. You should hear the music of heaven. You have personality traits as I do. You have the ability to feel compassion and to care for those less fortunate. Unfortunately, since the fall of man, some of you are capable of extreme cruelty. That is not from Me. None of My other created beings are like you. While I love them and provide for them, they cannot relate to Me like you.

[I] created [your] inmost being; [I] knit [you] together in [your] mother's womb. [My] eyes saw [your] unformed body.[110] Therefore, since each of you has been formed by Me and granted personalities and talents as I have chosen, be at peace with yourself and use these gifts to serve Me and others.

Lord, when You described the events of creation, You seem to be setting up six specific time periods of Your activity: creating light; separating the waters above from those below; forming dry grounds and bringing forth vegetation; clearing the sky for the sun, moon, and stars to appear: creating life in the waters and birds; and creating animals and humans.

You can describe it that way although some activities may have overlapped others.

How long did it take to complete each of these creation activities?

Some of these events took longer than others as you understand time but for me, a thousand years in [My] sight are like a day that has just gone by, or like a watch in the night.[111] Remember also that creating mankind was my last major act of creation and until then, there was no one to measure days or years.

I don't think I can remember all this as you have described in order to write it down.

Don't worry. When you are ready to write, I'll be with you to make sure that you cover the topics correctly and the manner I desire. But again, the steps or how I brought about creation is not the important point. Why I did is important and you will focus most of your attention on this area.

Thus the heavens and the earth were completed in all their vast array.[112] When I finished the work of creation, I rested but I'm still at work in the world as you well know. I set the example for you in that in the seventh period or day, I rested. This is a special time and as you know, it is a special day for you as well. You are to remember the Sabbath day by keeping it holy.[113] Even though I completed My work in creation, I am still at work in the world. I enjoy the times when people recognize My hand in their lives as I respond to their requests.

Why do Bad Things Happen to Good People?

This may be one of the toughest questions with which we wrestle because most of us have specific times when we have asked this of God directly. My brother-in-law was a volunteer fireman in Upstate New York and on the scene of a terrible accident on the Northway (I-87) where a six-year-old girl was killed. Why would God let such a bad thing happen to such an innocent person? She had been robbed of so much. He never found an answer that was satisfying. In our sense of justice, we are glad when a person is held accountable for the bad things that they do. But why does God allow the victims to suffer? And why does it seem that bad people prosper? So the converse question, why do good things happen to bad people? The book of Job is a great resource in the times of asking these questions. But just as Job wrestled with this question, I am certain that Moses did as well. Certainly, Moses would have had a discussion with God about it. Can we listen in to his discussion?

Moses: O God, our ancestor Dinah, the daughter of Jacob and Leah was raped by Shechem son of Hamor the Hivite.[114] Why did this happen to Dinah? Why did you allow this to happen? Why do bad things happen to good people?

Moses, we've discussed "good" before. For all have sinned and fall short of the glory of God.[115]

I think you know what I mean. Maybe a better word would be "innocent"? There are a lot of bad things in this world. The Ammonites sacrifice their children to their god, Molek. You have said, "Any Israelite or any foreigner residing in Israel who sacrifices any of his children to Molek is to be put to death."[116] Why would You even allow such things to enter the mind of people?

Okay, then, let's dig into this question. I know a defining question for many in years to come, "Would a loving God allow such a thing to happen?"

Moses, I designed a perfect world. The world I created, the one into which I brought Adam and Eve was a perfect world. [I] saw all that [I] had made, and it was very good.[117] My commands were understood there. The relationship I had with them was perfect. We walked and talked together. I put them there to work it and take care of it[118] but it was enjoyable and life was good. Adam and Eve changed all that when they disobeyed Me. I gave them the ability to choose to do what was right. I gave them the perfect world but I did not force them to obey Me. I love My people but I will not force them to obey.

But their disobedience was not their own idea. The serpent enticed them.

But they still had a choice. They did not have to choose the path they took. They could have resisted. But we really see here the sin was one of arrogance in that they listened to the serpent and then believed that they too could be gods in My place.

Could you not have created the garden without that tree? Why did that tree have to be there? Did it serve any other purpose than to deliberately tempt them?

Moses, until the serpent spoke with them, they had no problem with the tree. It was not a temptation because they had the right relationship with me. I said not to eat of it and that was not even a question. I don't think Eve had even looked at the fruit of that tree until she was tempted. When tempted, no one should say, "God is tempting me." For [I] cannot be tempted by evil, nor [do I] tempt anyone.[119] No, you cannot blame me for creating a trap for them. I created mankind with free will so that you can choose to do what is right.

So it is our free will that trips us up. Could you have eliminated that?

I desire a relationship with you that is based on love and faith. What kind of life would you have if I never allowed you to make choices? You would be little more than pets. Yes, I could have created the garden without that tree but Satan through that serpent or other means would have found another way to tempt them. But each person is tempted when they are dragged away by their own evil desire and enticed. Then, after desire has conceived, it gives birth to sin; and sin, when it is full-grown, gives birth to death.[120]

It was inevitable then that mankind would sin and be expelled from the perfect world.

As I said, I don't tempt people to sin. In every situation, you have the choice. No temptation has overtaken you except what is common to mankind. And [I] am faithful; [I] will not let you be tempted beyond what you can bear. But when you are tempted, [I] will also provide a way out so that you can endure it.[121] I desire that in every situation that you make the correct choice but I do not prevent you from making an incorrect choice. And every choice carries with it the consequences of making that choice.

So could you not have forgiven them their sin at that time and restored the relationship?

What was their reaction to being caught in this disobedience? They hid from Me. They blamed each other, they blamed the serpent. As you are implying now, you could be blaming Me. They were not repentant. No, their actions required that they face the consequences.

You have provided us a way for atonement. Could you not have provided that for them?

[My] works are perfect, and all [My] ways are just.[122] I told them what the consequences would be. I cannot fail in My justice. But I did not abandon them. I still had a relationship with them and with the others that followed. But this was a significant moment when Satan entered My creation.

Why not eliminate Satan then?

Satan will have his punishment but that is beyond your understanding and we won't discuss that here.

Okay, so bad things happened to Adam and Eve because of their disobedience.

Yes, and their sin changed mankind's relation with Me forever. Just as sin entered the world through one man, and death through sin, and in this way death came to all people, because all sinned.[123] That is one way that bad things happen. All should be held accountable for their bad choices and bad actions.

But what about Dinah? The rape happened to her. It wasn't her action that brought on that consequence.

That is correct. Believe me, I feel the pain and sorrow over her situation like I do for all things caused by improper human choices. It was the bad choice by Shechem son of Hamor the Hivite. He suffered the consequences of his sin later.

But Dinah was an innocent victim. What about her?

She is not responsible for what happened to her. She is innocent and you should not feel that because this bad thing happened that she shares in the blame. In this world you will have trouble.[124] Some of the trouble people have is what they do to themselves. Some of the trouble is what others do to you. My heart grieves for Dinah and other victims.

Could you not have stopped Shechem to spare Dinah?

Yes, but what would you have Me do?

Well, change Shechem's mind or change the circumstances.

Are you asking for this situation only or for all cases where rape may be considered?

No rape is good or acceptable so I guess I would ask for all cases.

Okay, well let's think about that. Rape involves not only sexual desire but bullying or domination. In Shechem's case, he was infatuated by her and really wanted her as his wife. I suppose I could eliminate the sexual desire in all males. Is that what you want?

No. We certainly wouldn't want that.

Okay, well you see where I'm going. I either change your ability for free will or I eliminate some select areas where you have choice.

Okay, maybe you eliminate the intent for rape where it may be found but keep everything else the same.

So what do you think about stealing? Should I eliminate the intent for stealing just like rape? Should I eliminate the intent to dishonor parents?

Well, it does seem to me that rape is more serious an offense than stealing and stealing is more of an offense than dishonoring parents.

You know my command against stealing and about honoring your parents. To me, stealing, dishonoring parents and rape are all sins. You are to be perfect, as I am perfect. An offense against any one of my commandments is an offense against them all. For whoever keeps the whole law and yet stumbles at just one point is guilty of breaking all of it.[125]

Taking this to all areas, you would then be removing all our intent to sin. You would remove all our ability to disobey your commandments. This would remove any free will.

Moses, I desire our relationship to be based on love, not control. But you do have the basics of a perfect society. If everyone kept all My commandments, wouldn't the world be a much better place to live?

It would but we know that we are incapable of obeying them all.

You are right. No one is able to obey me perfectly. So having Me stop bad behavior does not appear to appeal to you as a solution to the problem. Now it may be that I will stop bad behavior when I choose to do so. I can arrange situations for outcomes I choose. I prevented Joseph's brothers from killing him as they first discussed but I did not stop them from selling him into slavery. But why I may choose in some cases and not in others is not for you to know. For my thoughts are not your thoughts, neither are your ways my ways.[126] It may not be because one is more deserving than another. It is my choice. I will have mercy on whom I have mercy, and I will have compassion on whom I have compassion.[127]

Okay, let's talk then about death. I am old compared to the rest of the Israelites—more than sixty years older than most. We expect that older people will die but it seems so tragic when someone dies in their youth.

Do you think an older person is loved less by his or her family than a younger person?

No, I guess we would mourn the same but with an older person, we kind of expect that to occur.

What age then is acceptable for someone to die? Forty? Sixty? One hundred twenty?

That's not what I mean. It just seems that a person dying at say less than twenty-five years means that they will miss so much in life.

Yes, they may miss marriage, raising children and seeing children married but someone dying at fifty may also miss seeing children married, seeing grandchildren grow and other things. Life is meant to be enjoyed while it is available. I desire you to have life to the full.

I see that but a short life just seems such a tragedy.

Moses, it really depends on your perspective. Let me give you an example. Consider the distance from Egypt to Canaan where I am leading you. That is a long distance. Now, consider one foot. That one foot is almost nothing compared to the total distance. Now, consider one inch. That one inch is like the foot compared to the total distance. So looking at the entire journey, a foot is almost the same as an inch.

Now consider eternity. I am eternal. Life with Me is eternal. That is similar to the distance from Egypt to Canaan. Your life may be compared to the foot and a person dying young as compared to the inch. You would see your life to be twelve times as long as the youth or the youth has only one twelfth the length of life as you. But when compared to eternity, both are the same. That is my perspective. It is not for you to know what happens after your death other than I prepare for each person's place. So whether a person dies young or old, a place is prepared for them.

Are we all with you after death? What about those who reject you.

Let's save that discussion until later. I want us to continue to think about the time a person dies. So, if you are to look at it from My perspective, everyone will die and I have the ultimate authority over death. So it is no more tragic for a person to die young as to die old. But also know this, are not two sparrows sold for a penny? Yet not one of them will fall to the ground outside [My] care...you are worth more than many sparrows.[128]

But let's consider those who reject Me. To them, they only see life as a foot long. They don't see it as eternity. The shortness of their own life then would be tragic to them and the shortness of a youth dying would be more of a tragedy. For one who thinks their existence is only on this world and that is their only hope; that is indeed tragic. They will be greatly surprised when they stand before Me because people are destined to die once, and after that to face judgment.[129]

Sometimes people are injured or die, not because of someone else but because of earthquake, illness or accident. Whose fault is that?

This is not a perfect world anymore. I created a perfect world but because sin entered it and Satan has taken an interest here, it is no longer a perfect place. Illnesses happen. Disasters and accidents happen in the natural world. In this world, you will have trouble. Do not think that because someone is hurt through an event in the natural world that they are any more a sinner than others. If someone dies as a result of the disaster, that is My issue and I handle it. If someone is injured or incapacitated, it becomes a challenge for the individual. I would want them to seek Me in a close relationship to help get through that situation. For I am the Lord your God who takes hold of your right hand and says to you, Do not fear; I will help you.[130]

You may indeed be our only hope that when calamity strikes, we turn to You for help. When the plague broke out, you directed me to make a snake and when people looked at it, they did not die.

Sometimes My help will be that obvious but other times it may be more individualized so you don't know I'm at work. I am the Father of compassion and the God of all comfort.[131] There may be times that a person has a situation that I alone can mend. Just like I did with Pharaoh, there may be times that I act so that you may see My glory.

I don't know if this really answers my question. I understand that we don't live in a perfect world and that we are responsible for our actions or are hurt by the actions of others. To you, all life is precious but all life is Your responsibility. We mourn the bad things that happen to people that may not be a result of their own actions. It sounds like ultimately, there is no knowing the answer to this question for us. We simply need to love you, keep our relationship with You and trust You. When we call on you for help, You are there whether we feel it or not or if the situation changes or not. Even that is your choice. I know for certain that I can tell the Israelites, "The Lord himself goes before you and will be with you; he will never leave you nor forsake you, Do not be afraid; do not be discouraged."[132]

I do see that you have set before [us] life and death, blessings and curses. Now [I will tell the Israelites] to choose life, so that [we] and [our] children may live and that [we] may love the Lord [our] God, listen to [Your] voice, and hold fast to [You]. For the Lord is [our] life.[133]

GLIMPSE AHEAD

Numbers 27:12 - 36:13
Deuteronomy

A t the end of forty years of wandering in the desert, the Israelites were poised to take the land that God promised them. This time there was no hesitation or rebellion. They were camped in the area of Beth Peor on the east side of the Jordan River across from Jericho. They had systematically conquered the region east of the Jordan River from the Arnon River Gorge (east side of the Dead Sea or Salt Sea) north to Mount Herman near Damascus as the kings of these locations came to fight.

God directed Moses to take a census of all males of the age of twenty and older. The total was 601,730. The land they were taking was to be allotted to each of the twelve tribes based upon this census. The Levites were set apart to serve the Lord and were not allotted their own section of the land. However, four hundred years earlier as Jacob was near the end of his life, his son Joseph brought his two sons Ephraim and Manasseh to Jacob. Jacob blessed them and said, "May they be called by my name and the names of my fathers Abraham and Isaac…"[1] and thus, Jacob effectively adopted Joseph's sons as his own and the tribe of Joseph became the half tribe of Ephraim and half tribe of Manasseh so the land was to be divided into these twelve tribes.

In this camp, the leaders of the tribes of Reuben and Gad approached Moses with the request that their allotted land be that on the east side of the Jordan that had just been taken in battle. Moses agreed with the condition that these tribes would continue to fight with the other tribes as they conquered the rest of the land west of the Jordon. They agreed and the land was given to them and to the half tribe of Manasseh.

The census revealed nearly the same number of men as there were when leaving Egypt although all that generation of them had died along the way, as God had required, except Caleb and Joshua. That meant that the oldest of the Israelites, other than Moses, Caleb, and Joshua would have been sixty years old or younger. All who were older than twenty at the start of the Exodus forty years earlier died. Caleb and Joshua were allowed to cross into the land because only they of the twelve spies urged the Israelites to take the land when first directed by God to do so.

As was suggested in the First Forty Years chapter, the entire population of Israelites at this time would have been about the same as leaving Egypt at between 2 and 2.5 million people.

It is interesting to note that when Jacob's family first arrived in Egypt about 450 years prior to this time, there were about seventy-five persons in the family. When God first promised Abraham that He would give the land to Abraham and his descendants, there would have been little that Abraham could have done with such a small force to take the land. Nor could he have held it with his small family. However, God provided the intervening years to grow the family into a large nation that was then a formidable force. God announced to Moses at this time that, "This very day I will begin to put the terror and fear of you on all the nations under heaven. They will hear reports of you and will tremble and be in anguish because of you."[2]

However, Moses was not to lead them in for his own failures recorded in Numbers 20:2–12. He was 120 years old at the time and although fit enough to climb a mountain, Joshua was selected by God for this leading role. Joshua had been an aide to Moses for most of the journey. He was mentioned as an aide shortly after leaving Egypt[3] and led the Israelites in battle. Joshua and Caleb were the only spies to encourage the Israelites to take the land the first time they were directed to do so by God.

The book of Deuteronomy provides a summary of their travels and final discourses by Moses as he exhorts the Israelites to be faithful to God. God is about to deliver on His promise to them to give them the land promised to Abraham nearly seven hundred years earlier. The Lord appeared to Abram [Abraham] and said, "To your offspring I will give this land."[4] Moses repeatedly clearly spells out two potential outcomes for the Israelites: "See, I am setting before you today a blessing and a curse—the blessing if you obey the commands of the Lord your God that I am giving you today; the curse if you disobey the commands of the Lord your God and turn from the way that I command you today."[5]

Although Moses was not allowed to lead the Israelites into the promised land, God did show him the land from the top of Mount Nebo. Moses climbed the mountain and after seeing the promised land, died in the presence of God and God buried him there. He was 120 years old, yet his eyes were not weak nor his strength gone.[6]

At the end of the book of Deuteronomy, it is reiterated that Moses, whom the Lord knew face to face…[7] had this special relationship with God. After spending forty years talking with God face-to-face, what final questions may Moses have had? Perhaps these were some of the topics of conversation.

Leadership

At several points early in this journey, Moses's leadership is challenged. While the first time it was questioned was after Moses's first visit with Pharaoh and Pharaoh increased their burden, it was shortly after leaving their slave homes at the Red Sea that they again complained to Moses. This occurred again over difficulty in finding water, food, food other than manna, the golden calf, and several other events. There is no question that God was leading His people to the promised land but God chose Moses to be His representative, His leader in accomplishing this task. Today, there are a myriad of books on leadership; each having its prescription on what characteristics or traits are exhibited by a good leader. Leadership traits displayed by Moses included establishing authority, setting the vision, delegating authority, providing resources, providing consistency, caring for the people, maintaining discipline, communicating well, and completing the mission. How did Moses view this leadership role?

Moses: Lord, this has been a very fulfilling time for me. As I view my life, I see three forty-year periods. The first forty were quite carefree. I enjoyed the pleasures of the palace in Egypt. They were easy times for me and I was honored as a potential heir of the Pharaoh. I learned much and was well educated but there wasn't a purpose for me. I didn't see a future with the Egyptians and didn't know where to go with that. I then rashly killed the Egyptian and had to flee. The next forty years were very lonely. Even though I married, I felt I had no purpose in this life. Then You called me to lead Your people out of slavery in Egypt to this promised land. Suddenly, and I mean very suddenly, I had a purpose and a place. You placed me into leadership and it has been difficult but greatly rewarding. I have been honored by You in this and since You have directed me to write about it, others will honor me in the future.

Moses, I saw your heart. Even though you had not demonstrated any real leadership except for those sheep, I saw character that was what I wanted.

You may have wanted it but it was hard to convince the people that it was what they would accept.

One of your first questions, Moses, was whether the people would accept you. You said, "What if they do not believe me or listen to me and say, 'The Lord did not appear to you.'"[8] You learned from your first experience that you had no credibility on your own. You needed to have some authority to assume the leadership role.

Without You leading us, no one would have followed me.

This was a situation unlike any other. There is a succession line for the Pharaoh and for kings. But this was a new position. Your authority had to be established.

I had no authority except that it came from You. I didn't gain the leadership position by birthright, wealth, or physical, political, or military strength. I could not promote myself into this role. I was a total outsider. I didn't even grow up with them. The Israelites had their tribal leaders but you were not promoting from within. They needed to know that [You] sent me to do all these things and that it was not my idea.[9] They needed to be convinced that You were bestowing this authority on me.

Yes, there is no authority except that which [I have] established.[10] Each time you were confronted, you correctly came to me. You did not try to mount a defense or argue with them that you should be the leader. When an arrogant person takes a leadership role, their arrogance will be evident and they will have to fight to keep their position. Others will want to depose them. In your humility, you were willing to follow Me, knowing that I would sustain you and you did not have to fight for your position. You let me affirm you.

Aaron and I told them they are not grumbling against us, but against the Lord.[11] After all, we were just being obedient to what You directed. Most of the time, they grumbled and complained about their conditions but there were times that they actually rebelled.

It is hard to understand their rebellion. My cloud was over the tabernacle by day, and fire was in the cloud by night, in the sight of all the Israelites during all their travels.[12] They knew I was there with you.

Your presence was essential for me and for our travel. I know you were very angry after the golden calf incident and said you would provide an angel to lead us. I knew we could not survive as a people if You did that. How will anyone know that you are pleased with me and with your people unless you go with us?[13]

You were quite insistent. You said, "If your Presence does not go with us, do not send us up from here." You were right and I agreed because I was pleased with you and knew you by name.

You gave me a huge task. You told me that You were sending me to Pharaoh to bring my people the Israelites out of Egypt.[14] You mentioned that [You] have promised to bring [them] up out of [their] misery in Egypt into the land of the Canaanites, Hittites, Amorites, Perizzites, Hivites and Jebuites—a land flowing with milk and honey[15] but you did not tell me that I was going to lead them there. So my focus was on obeying Your direction and completing this mission. The sign you provided was fulfilled. You said, "When you have brought the people out of Egypt, you will worship God on this mountain"[16]—the mountain on which we were standing. It came to be as You said.

Moses, you did not know Me well then. I could not give you the entire picture as you were just starting to follow Me. In fact, at the first resistance by Pharaoh and he increased the burden on the Israelites, you wavered. You questioned me in selecting you. You said to Me, "Why, Lord, why have you brought trouble on this people? Is this why you sent me? Ever since I went to Pharaoh to speak in your name, he has brought trouble on this people, and you have not rescued your people at all."[17] You thought it was going to be easy. How could I reveal all the difficulties you would encounter? You had enough of a task in doing this.

Lord, you said to me that you had hardened Pharaoh's heart so that [You] may perform these signs of yours among them that [we] may tell [our] children and grandchildren how [You] dealt harshly with the Egyptians and how [You] performed [Your] signs among them and that [we] may know that [You] are the Lord.[18] That truly happened to me. I came to know You and Your power through that experience. As a nation, we worshipped You after you rescued us through the Red Sea but it wasn't until we reached Mount Sinai that You revealed Your plans for us in the covenant we made. I had been leading the people out of Egypt and that task was completed. You now created a new vision for us: Out of all nations

[we] will be [your] treasured possession…and a holy nation.[19] You then gave us Your commands and honored me in front of all the Israelites by speaking directly to me. You said, "I am going to come to you in a dense cloud, so that the people will hear me speaking with you and will always put their trust in you."[20] In that way, You again affirmed me in my leadership role. I then had a new vision and mission: to lead the Israelites in keeping their covenant with You and to lead them into the land You had promised.

Now you knew Me. You spent time with Me when I gave you My commands and directions. You knew how to talk with Me and what to expect from Me. You had experienced My frustration with you before and you were beginning to see My whole personality.

This was a time of real growth for me. I was getting to know You at the same time that I was getting to know the Israelites. I had not known either before this time.

You grasped the leadership role of the Israelites very quickly. While you were with Me on the mountain for forty days and receiving My instruction, the Israelites broke with their promise to Me and began to worship the golden calf. I was angry and told you to leave me alone so that my anger may burn against them and that I may destroy them. Then I [would] make you into a great nation.[21] I could have done this and still kept my promises to Abraham, Isaac, and Jacob. You, their descendant, would have been the father of this great nation. However, you quickly interceded with Me for these people. You stood in the gap for them with Me.

You were gracious to listen to me and gracious to them and to relent. They were punished for their sin but You did not destroy them. You again were going to destroy them after their rebellion against taking the land.

You interceded for them and asked Me to forgive them, which I did. You stood in the breach before [Me] to keep [My] wrath from destroying them.[22] Again, they were punished but not destroyed. You really did care for them even though you hardly knew them.

I did get frustrated with their grumbling though. I remember saying to you, "Did I conceive all these people? Did I give them birth? I cannot carry all these people by myself; the burden is too heavy for me."[23]

You were right in taking this to Me. I don't intend that obedience to Me and your leadership would be too much for you. I provided you with a plan that included the tribal leaders. I said I would take some of the power of the Spirit that is on you and put it on them. They will share the burden of the people with you so that you will not have to carry it alone.[24] Jethro also provided you with ideas on how you could delegate authority and responsibility in settling disputes. However, you retained the overall leadership and all issues that could not be resolved by others were brought to you.

You were gracious to us, Lord. You gave us victory in battle and steered us clear of conflict when You determined it better for us.

You did well in maintaining discipline, Moses. When the tribes of Gad and Reuben came to you to ask for the land east of the Jordan, they were already prepared to join their fellows in the battles to come on the western side of the Jordan. They knew that you would require this of them before they asked.

Lord, one of the other missions You gave me was to write down what You directed. This was so to provide a record of these events but also to provide a witness to future generations of Your power and favor, Your love and care, Your commands and promises.

You finished writing in a book the words of this law from beginning to end[25] and have set that book in a place near the ark where it will remain as a witness. It will also be a means of grace for people for many years because faith comes from hearing the message.[26] I will add to this message in years to come as I determine to increase the faith of many for years to come.

Moses, you did well in completing the mission I set before you. The people are ready to enter the land I promised for them. But you were clear to them that it was because of My promise that they were going to take possession of the land. You said, "It is not because of your righteousness or your integrity that you are going in to take possession of their land; but on account of the wickedness of these nations, the Lord your God will drive them out before you, to accomplish what he swore to your fathers, to Abraham, Isaac and Jacob."[27] In fact, you were very clear in communicating all that I desired so that there is no question remaining. You have clearly shown them the blessings in obeying my commands and the curses if they do not.

Lord, I feel I have fulfilled my duty to [You] in all good conscience to this day.[28]

Moses, one of the traits that I saw in you from the beginning was humility. As I said, I look at the heart of people. When pride comes, then comes disgrace, but with humility comes wisdom.[29] Humility is the fear of the Lord.[30] The fear of the Lord is the beginning of wisdom, and knowledge of the Holy One is understanding.[31] Your humility was not false in pretending to be humble. You were sincere.

Lord, you directed me to write, "Moses was a very humble man, more humble than anyone else on the face of the earth."[32] I didn't want to write that but You directed it.

And it was appropriate to do so. You sought no rights or glory for yourself. You pointed to Me in all you did. Your words show great knowledge and understanding.

Loneliness/Aloneness

I wonder if Moses was a lonely man. Charles Swindoll suggests that although Moses died alone, loneliness is not the correct word: it should be aloneness.

> Not its loneliness, but its aloneness—there's a difference. Loneliness suggests an empty longing, reaching in vain for someone else. Aloneness means nobody else goes along.[33]

I look at Moses' life and for the first forty years, he is torn between living in the courts of Pharaoh and identifying with his fellow Israelites. He cannot associate with these slaves or risk his position with Pharaoh. He knew his parents and brother, Aaron, and sister, Miriam, but it does not appear that he was socially active with them. He was an outsider to the Israelites as evidenced by them informing the Pharaoh when he killed the Egyptian. Although he lives with the Egyptians, he doesn't really adopt them as his identity because he eventually sides with the Israelites. He runs for his life alone to Midian.

In Midian, he marries but spends his life as a shepherd. As such, he would be alone or perhaps with a small group, most of the time. At the burning bush, there is no evidence that anyone else was with him. He does have two sons born to Zipporah and him while in Midian but when hard times came on the journey back to Egypt; Zipporah and he have a falling out and he sends her and his sons back to her father. He is alone when he meets his brother Aaron on the way to Egypt.

Moses's father-in-law brings Zipporah and sons to him in the desert but the biblical account is totally about Jethro and nothing is said about Zipporah. In fact, Zipporah is not mentioned again until Aaron and Miriam complain about her. In this account, Moses does not call her by name and we don't hear of her again. While Moses records the death of Aaron and Miriam, he does not discuss the death of Zipporah, if in fact she did precede him in death. He was forty years old when he met her and she would likely have been near twenty years old so when Moses was 120, she would have been about 100, if living. As he climbs the mountain where he will die, he is again alone.

Moses was also separated from the Israelites with the veil that he wore. Whenever he entered the Lord's presence to speak with him, he removed the veil until he came out. And when he came out and told the Israelites what he had been commanded, they saw that his face was radiant. Then Moses would put the veil back over his face until he went in to speak with the Lord.[34] This veil would be a physical barrier and perhaps a social barrier between Moses and the rest of the Israelites. Moses's closest family members were his brother and sister but there was stress there as seen when they talked against him about his wife. Joshua was his closest aide throughout the journey.

Not only was the veil a separation from the Israelites but his age would have been another difference. When he was 120 years old, every other male other than Joshua and Caleb would have been sixty or less.

Family was very important to the Israelites. Families lived together as part of their tribe. There would likely have been a lot of interaction between family members. They would have been closely connected. Today, too, people are very connected in social relationships and social media. However, loneliness or aloneness is quite an issue. Through the difficult times in life, is there someone close by to go along? Assuming Moses felt alone, how may he have addressed this with God?

Moses: Lord, at your direction, I wrote in Genesis that You said, "It is not good for the man to be alone. I will make a helper suitable for him."[35] Aloneness is difficult for anyone. I have often had to go alone. I can easily share Your commands and direction but it is difficult to share with anyone much of what we discuss on a personal level.

Yes, Moses. I didn't just desire that people would have others around them but that for each there would be a "suitable helper." That is, someone who could help navigate the difficult times in life. Two are better than one, because they have a good return for their labor: If either of them falls down, one can help the other up. But pity and one who falls and has no one to help them up. Also, if two lie down together, they will keep warm. But how can one keep warm alone?[36] I don't just mean physically falling or keeping warm but also emotionally or mentally as well. A helper doesn't always mean a wife or husband. At times, a suitable helper could be a close friend.

I think I've missed a lot by not having close friends. I don't mean to minimize our time together. I so appreciate You being so close that we can talk as friends. Still, Aaron has been very busy so I guess Joshua is about the closest friend that I have. I certainly didn't have any close friends in Egypt. There was no one in whom I could confide. In Midian, I guess Jethro was a friend even though he was my father-in-law. Still, I could not confide in him the experience with You at Mt. Sinai.

Friends are helpful. Though one may be overpowered, two can defend themselves. A cord of three strands is not quickly broken.[37] There is strength in having close friends. It is a lot easier to stand up to the difficulties of life when there are others with you to support you. They can also hold you accountable for your actions. When you may be tempted to break one of My commands, confide in friends who can then support you against that temptation.

Joshua was always a faithful friend. Aaron was close to me most of the time also. You often spoke to both of us. When there was difficulty with the people, both of us went from the assembly to the entrance to the tent of meeting and fell facedown[38] where Your glory appeared to us.

When looking for friends, you must beware. The righteous choose their friends carefully, but the way of the wicked leads them astray.[39] Therefore, seek to have friends among the believers. You were right to be cautious of the Egyptians. They could have easily led you astray and advised you to marry an Egyptian. Jethro may have understood but until he heard the stories of My signs in Egypt, he may not have been helpful to you. I'd also say, do not make friends with a hot-tempered person, do not associate with one easily angered, or you may learn their ways and get yourself ensnared.[40]

I was alone most of the forty years in Midian. There was no one around then when I was out with the sheep. I was in some lonely places far from home.

I know Moses, I was watching. You didn't know Me but I knew you.

But many feel alone even if there are others around. I felt alone in Pharaoh's court since they were not my people. We live in tribes here but still some feel alone without an intimate friend. Some things are just too intimate to share with someone who isn't that close and connected. I think about Lot and his family living in Sodom. Ten righteous people could not be found there.[41] Lot didn't have a lot in common with them.

Still, Lot's wife was sorry to leave that city. Don't be misled: "Bad company corrupts good character."[42] She could have swayed him to become like the rest of the people there. But you are right that a friend loves at all times, and a brother is born for a time of adversity.[43]

The really hard times, the times of adversity are when we need close friends the most. For me, there wasn't much I could do to look for close friends either in Egypt or shepherding the sheep.

You were in difficult situations. For most when looking for friends who will not lead them astray, they should look to the community of believers first. The fear of the Lord is the beginning of wisdom[44] and this is where the true friends will be found. Even when you were at home in Midian, there weren't many who believed first in Me. In the community of believers, you must love one another. But love must be sincere. Hate what is evil; cling to what is good.[45] Who is wise and understanding among you? Let them show it by their good life, by deeds done in the humility that comes from wisdom.[46] People will see the good works. People will be noticed in doing this. Seek friends who are doing good deeds from their hearts. As iron sharpens iron, so one person sharpens another.[47] Likewise, the lonely person who is doing My will is going to find fulfillment in this. At the same time, they may be noticed by others. You may find close friends who share in the good work.

I've felt alone doing Your work. Others don't understand the work load or necessarily the weight of the load. Zipporah didn't understand why I didn't have much time for her with all the people depending on me.

Moses, a leader in serving Me is in a different situation. Not everyone can understand the difficulties in carrying out My desires. The leader is to be above reproach, faithful to his wife, temperate, self-controlled, respectable, hospitable, able to teach, not given to drunkenness, not violent but gentle, nor quarrelsome, not a lover of money. He must manage his own family well and see that his children obey him, and he must do so in a manner worthy of full respect.[48] I hold the leaders and teachers more accountable because you know that [those] who teach will be judged more strictly.[49]

It is that higher accountability that can be the source of family conflict. I know what You require. It is my responsibility to relate that to the people and lead them. There is no one else You have called to do this. I cannot simply stop or take a break because there is no one else.

Look at what you are doing to see if there are ways that you can share part of the responsibility with others. Jethro provided good advice when he suggested you select capable men from all the people—men who fear [Me], trustworthy men who hate dishonest gain—and appoint them as officials[50] to help you. You are still responsible and need to train and supervise them but they can carry much of the load with you. That also provides others the opportunity to show leadership and to serve Me.

I agree. Still, I have the final responsibility and it can be difficult to try to gain balance between doing Your work and relating to our families. We need to manage our family relationships and carry out Your instructions.

When this causes stress for you, lean on Me. Those who hope in [Me] will renew their strength. They will soar on wings like eagles; they will run and not grow weary, they will walk and not be faint.[51] At the same time, you should listen to those around you and really take note of their input. The way of fools seems right to them, but the wise listen to advice. Fools show their annoyance at once, but the prudent overlook an insult.[52] What is said may not be intended as an insult but actually be good advice. Nevertheless, you may also receive some very bad advice and not all comments from others will be helpful.

I do hear a lot of comments and advice. I am your servant; give me discernment that I may understand your statutes[53] and test the advice I receive.

You can also take these comments to Me. Cast your cares on [Me] and [I] will sustain you. [I] will never let the righteous be shaken.[54]

I know You have been very good to me and I really enjoy our time together. This is an incredible and unique situation. I am honored that You speak to me as a friend. Who am I that I should be this close to you as were Abraham, Isaac and Jacob? Still, I desire someone's personal touch.

I know that humans desire the personal and emotional attachment with another human. Even though Adam and I had a very close relationship in the Garden, I knew that I was not the suitable helper for him. He needed someone like him to be his companion.

Lord, I don't mean to complain about this. There are times when solitude is important. I've appreciated our times of solitude. Spending forty days with you on Mt. Sinai was not a lonely time for me but a time of great revelation and joy in discovering more about you.

There are times when I call you to come with me by yourselves to a quiet place and get some rest.[55] This can be a time of renewal.

Is it your plan that there is someone for everyone with whom they can share intimate moments and thoughts? Is there a wife or husband for everyone?

People need to be careful in looking for a spouse. I have told you that for those living around you, do not intermarry with them. Do not give your daughters to their sons or take their daughters for your sons.[56] Do not be yoked together with unbelievers. For what do righteousness and wickedness have in common?[57] So exercise good judgment when considering a husband or wife.

Suppose one finds themselves in a relationship with an unbeliever, what should they do?

First, they must keep My commands. Do not participate in any detestable practices. If any believer has a wife who is not a believer and she is willing to live with him, he must not divorce her. And if a woman has a husband who is not a believer and he is willing to live with her, she must not divorce him.[58] Being willing to live with the other means that they do not find obedience to Me to be objectionable nor will they interfere with worship and devotion to Me. Woe to those who call evil good and good evil, who put darkness for light and light for darkness, who put bitter for sweet and sweet for bitter.[59] If you act in love, as I have commanded you, with your husband or wife, you may be light in their darkness.

There are times of aloneness in life. A widow or orphan doesn't choose to be alone. Sometimes one cannot find the suitable helper.

The Lord is close to the brokenhearted and saves those who are crushed in spirit.[60] You can write for all people, The Lord himself goes before you and will be with you; he will never leave you nor forsake you. Do not be afraid; do not be discouraged."[61]

Be Holy

It was forty years before this that Moses first heard the word *holy* related to God. At the burning bush, God said, "Take off your sandals, for the place where you are standing is holy ground."[62] When giving Moses the commands and instructions, God said several times that they were to be holy because God is holy. They must not have fully understood this because in the first couple of years in the desert, they complained and rebelled against God several times. God had to discipline them severely each time. But now as they are ready to take the land He promised, they had a much better idea of what it meant for them. They had been obedient to God as He gave them direction to approach the promised land and each time they formed for battle, God gave them the victory. God had truly set them apart for Himself. He was their God and they were His people. This may have been a topic of conversation during these forty years and it may have gone something like this.

Moses: Lord, we are camped across the Jordan from the land you promised us. During these forty years, we have learned much about what it means to be Your people. In the early days, many people complained or rebelled and wanted to go back to Egypt but they have not done so for a long time. You told us, "I am the Lord who brought you up out of Egypt to be your God; therefore be holy because I am holy."[63] We are a people who are sincerely trying to be obedient and to be holy by keeping your commands.

For you are a people holy to [Me] your God. [I have] chosen you out of all the peoples on the face of the earth to be [My] people, [My] treasured possession.[64]

The people in the promised land know this too. As You promised, You have put the terror and fear of [us] on the whole land, wherever [we] go.[65]

Moses, I want you to call the people together to review what you have been through and stress to them the importance of My commands and that they must be careful to follow them in the land that I have given them. Tell them, "Love the Lord your God and keep his requirements, his decrees, his laws and his commands always."[66]

Lord, I have been telling them this. I will say it again, several times. I know that they listen to me because they know You talk to me and I am telling them what You say and command. But You also know that they have been rebellious against [You] ever since I have known [them].[67]

Moses, you will recall that I placed no conditions on the people in order to free them from their slavery. They did not have to fight against the Egyptians, they did not have to vow allegiance to Me, nothing. It was by My grace and My promise to Abraham, Isaac and Jacob that I acted. In the Desert of Sinai three months after leaving Egypt, I said, "Now if you obey me fully and keep my covenant, then out of all nations you will be my treasured possession. Although the whole earth is mine, you will be for me a kingdom of priests and a holy nation."[68] The people all agreed. I commanded you: Do not profane my holy name, for I must be acknowledged as holy by the Israelites.[69] They are a holy nation and must be holy because I am holy. You told them, "Be holy because I, the Lord your God, am holy."[70]

I told them everything you commanded me to tell them.

So then, they know that to remain in this covenant relationship with Me, they must keep my commands and decrees. They must be holy. If a person sins and does what is forbidden in any of the Lord's commands, even though he does not know it, he is guilty and will be held responsible.[71] Moses, what is the penalty for sinning against My commands?

It is a broken relationship with You and separation from You as it was for Adam. The wages of sin is death[72]—eternal separation from You and You will blot out their names from under heaven.[73] You have also told us what will happen to us as a nation if we turn from You. I have warned them of the calamities that will befall them.

So, if someone desires to restore the right relationship with Me, what do they do?

In Your grace, You have provided a way for them to restore that relationship with you. Making a commitment to try harder is not enough. It is not enough that they do good things. It is not enough that they express sorrow over their sin. It is not enough that they confess their sin. Without the shedding of blood there is no forgiveness.[74] They must offer a sin offering.

Yes, and if that offering is a lamb, it shall be without defect. They are to lay their hand on its head and slaughter it.[75] By placing their hand on its head, they are recognizing that this animal is innocent of their sin and is taking their place in substitutionary death. Then they will be forgiven[76] and the relationship with Me is restored. For the life of a creature is in the blood, and I have given it to you to make atonement for yourselves on the altar; it is the blood that makes atonement for one's life.[77] If they are disturbed that an innocent lamb is slaughtered for them, they should be and recognize the seriousness of their sin.

You have also commanded us to make atonement once a year for all the sins of the Israelites.[78] I thank You on behalf of all the Israelites that You have provided a way for us to remain in a right relationship with You.

Okay. Then you must purge the evil from Israel.[79] You must purge the evil intents and actions of the people who live there as well as any within the Israelite nation. You must purge away false witnesses,[80] the guilt of shedding innocent blood,[81] showing contempt for the judge or priest who stands ministering there to the LORD your God,[82] rebellious sons,[83] kidnapping,[84] promiscuity,[85] false prophets,[86] and other actions that can lead people away from Me. Then all Israel will hear and be afraid, and no one among you will do such an evil thing again.[87]

Lord, You showed us this by example when in the desert. There were those who rebelled or complained against You, but You purged them from our midst or showed all the people their error in a way they could not forget.

Lord, I have asked them again these forty years later and again they agreed. I told them clearly, "You have declared this day that the Lord is your God and that you will walk in obedience to him, that you will keep his decrees, commands and laws—that you will listen to him. And the Lord has declared this day that you are his people, his treasured possession as he promised, and that you are to keep all his commands. He has declared that he will set you in praise, fame and honor high above all the nations he has made and that you will be a people holy to the Lord your god, as he promised."[88]

God's Work

On the seventh day of creation, God rested from His work of creation but God remains at work today. The Lord works righteousness and justice for all the oppressed.[89] We see from the Bible that God has emotions that are imaged in us. I would suspect that God's work is similar to what we do in that some brings enjoyment and other work is a duty that needs to be done. We know that as for God, his way is perfect[90] and His work is perfect. But is there work He does that particularly brings Him joy and enjoyment? As a friend, would Moses have broached this subject?

Moses: Lord, you are my God; I will exalt you and praise your name, for in perfect faithfulness you have done wonderful things, things planned long ago.[91] I look at the mighty works that You have done from creation to now and am amazed at what You do. I witnessed Your work in Egypt. Your work is serious work. You are holy and serious about holiness and about the holiness of Your people.

Is there work You do that brings You special delight; that You really enjoy?

I really enjoy relating to My people. [I] take[s] delight in [my] people; [I] crown the humble with victory.[92] [I] am love. Whoever lives in love lives in [Me], and [I] in them.[93] Certainly there are those who acknowledge Me and try to obey Me but I enjoy those who especially love Me. I take delight in those who fear [Me], who put their hope in [My] unfailing love.[94] Take delight in [Me] and [I] will give you the desires of your heart.[95]

How can we take delight in You?

Oh, I know when people take delight in Me. I know their hearts. They show their delight in various ways and I enjoy their praise. There are those who say, "I will be glad and rejoice in you; I will sing the praises of your name, O Most High."[96] Some are not able to contain the joy in this relationship. I hear, "Shout for joy to the Lord, all the earth, burst into jubilant song with music."[97]

There are some who know You and seek to keep Your commands but don't necessarily show "delight" in You.

They are still My people and I love them. You know how to give good gifts to your children, how much more will [I] give good gifts to those who ask [Me].[98] They are missing out on much.

You are holy and expect us to be holy but we do sin against you.

So I enjoy repentance. There is rejoicing in the presence of the angles of God over one sinner who repents.[99] When people recognize their error and foolishness of this world and turn to Me, I rejoice. Some are convinced that belief in Me is foolishness or a personal weakness. The foolishness of God is wiser than human wisdom, and the weakness of God is stronger than human strength.[100] I will destroy the wisdom of the wise; the intelligence of the intelligent I will frustrate.[101] But I will give wisdom; from [My] mouth come knowledge and understanding.[102]

What can we do that pleases You?

You cannot achieve righteousness or be acceptable to Me without acknowledging your sin and seeking forgiveness no matter how many good things that you do. But, when you are in a right relationship with Me, I enjoy seeing generosity and humility. Whoever sows sparingly will also reap sparingly, and whoever sows generously will also reap generously.[103] Your generosity will result in thanksgiving to [Me].[104] All the arrogant and every evildoer will be stubble, and the day that is coming will set them on fire.[105] But, clothe yourselves with humility toward one another, because, [I] oppose the proud but show favor to the humble.[106] For those who exalt themselves will be humbled, and those who humble themselves will be exalted.[107]

I also enjoy people who can see and acknowledge My work. Blessed are the pure in heart, for they will see [Me].[108] If you look for My actions and work in this world, you will see Me. I am at work all around you in caring for My people. In all things [I] work for the good of those who love [Me], who have been called according to [My] purpose.[109] I like to grant favor and blessings to people also, especially when they think it is impossible. When she became pregnant at a very old age, Abraham wife Sarah said, 'God has brought me laughter, and everyone who hears about this will laugh with me."[110] You may think something impossible. With man this is impossible, but not with [Me]; all things are possible with [Me].[111]

Another thing I truly enjoy is seeing people work in the gifts I give them. Each of you has your own gift from [Me]; one has this gift, another has that.[112] I myself have selected your fellow Levites from among the Israelites as a gift to you...to do the work at the tent of meeting.[113] When it came to the tabernacle, I gave skill and ability to know how to carry out all the work of constructing the tabernacle.[114] You are all created in My image as we talked about before. So when you work at the gifts and aspects of My personality and excel, I am pleased. If your gift is in the arts, then work at singing, dancing, sculpture, carving and so forth. When you plant your vineyards, when you tend your sheep, when you work in wood, when you write, when you consider the universe, whatever you do, work at it with all your heart, as working for the Lord.[115] This is pleasing to Me.

How about our sacrifices? Are they pleasing to You?

Yes, sacrifices that are offered with a true heart and in keeping with a right relationship with Me, are an aroma pleasing to [Me].[116] People who make personal sacrifices in serving others and put their religion into practice…this is pleasing to [Me].[117]

Do you enjoy Your creation?

Moses, when I finished creation and I saw all I had made, it was very good.[118] Yes. I enjoy My creation in the way that I created it. Things are not the same since Adam and Eve sinned against Me but parts of My creation remain. Lift up your eyes and look to the heavens…I bring out the starry host one by one and call forth each of them by name.[119] I watch the sunrises and sunsets. I watch the baby animals play. I know when the mountain goats give birth…I watch when the doe bears her fawn.[120] The wings of the ostrich flap joyfully, though they cannot compare with the wings and feathers of the stork.[121] I love to look on the cedars of Lebanon. Every animal of the forest is mine, and the cattle on a thousand hills. I know every bird in the mountains, and the insects in the fields are mine.[122] Yes, I still enjoy My creation and My people.

Lord, May these words of my mouth and this meditation of my heart be pleasing in your sight, Lord, my Rock and my Redeemer.[123]

The Future

God told Moses that he would not enter the promised land but he has been leading them for forty years. As Moses nears the time of his death, he would naturally look ahead to what God has in mind for His people.

Moses: Lord, I am about to go the way of my ancestors. What can you tell me about what lies ahead for these Your people?

Moses, as you know, Joshua will lead the people into the land I promised. He will be strong and courageous. [I] will drive out those nations before [him], little by little. [He] will not be allowed to eliminate them all at once, or the wild animals will multiply around you.[124] And he will divide out the land for the twelve tribes and they will occupy the land.

But they will not hold fast to their promises to You, will they?

They will for a time but no, these people will soon prostitute themselves to the foreign gods of the land they are entering. They will forsake me and break the covenant I made with them...Many disasters and calamities will come on them...I know what they are disposed to do, even before I bring them into the land I promised them on oath.[125]

I told them that this would happen to them. I even told them that they would be dispersed among the nations. But even when that happens I said, "When you and your children return to the Lord your God and obey him will all your heart and with all your soul according to everything I command you today, then the Lord your God will restore your fortunes and have compassion on you and gather you again from all the nations where he scattered you."[126] Knowing this ahead of time should be a caution for them but I know it won't.

I have written the book as You directed. After I finished it, I gave this command to the Levites, "Take this Book of the Law and place it beside the ark of the covenant of the Lord your God. There it will remain as a witness against you...For I know that after my death you are sure to become utterly corrupt and turn from the way I have commanded you."[127] Will it be read? Will it be of value to those who follow?

Moses, this is the start of scripture. Others will add their story and experiences to what you have written. I will lead them in what to write so that all scripture...is useful for teaching, rebuking, correcting and training in righteousness.[128] It will be a blessing for countless people.

Lord, I have come to know You a lot better than what I have written at Your direction. Do you not want me to include more of our personal discussions? Won't that help people also?

Moses, like you, I desire people to seek a more personal relationship with Me where I can reveal myself to them individually. This gets to a much deeper friendship and realization of My direct involvement in their lives. That won't develop by hearing of someone else's personal relationship but through development of their own. To those who seek this relationship, I will respond and they will know Me.

I have found you, Lord, are forgiving and good, abounding in love to all who call to you.[129]

You have also revealed to me that after they are in the land, the people will want a king. I have told them how the king should be chosen by You. I have given them many warnings about a king as well. He must be from among your fellow Israelites…he must not acquire great numbers of horses for himself…he must not take many wives…he must not accumulate large amounts of silver and gold… and he is to write for himself on a scroll a copy of this law…and he is to read it all the days of his life.[130] He needs to do these things so that he will follow You and not be led astray. Are they going to heed this warning?

For a short time, Moses, but they will turn from this advice. These are things to come that you need not be concerned about. You have done what I asked of you.

But I want to address some other things You have revealed to me. When Adam and Eve sinned, you said to the serpent, "I will put enmity between you and the woman, and between your offspring and hers; he will crush your head, and you will strike his heel."[131] You appear to be telling us that someone in the future will come to crush the serpent, Satan.

You have also said that you will raise up prophets. At Horeb you told me, "I will raise up for them a prophet like you from among their fellow Israelites, and I will put my words in his mouth. He will tell them everything I command him. I myself will call to account anyone who does not listen to my words that the prophet speaks in my name.[132]

Then, when Jacob is old and near death, he blesses his children. Of Judah he says, "The scepter will not depart from Judah, nor the ruler's staff from between his feet, until he to whom it belongs shall come and the obedience of the nations shall be his."[133] Here again, You appear to be talking of the future, of the offspring of Judah. It sounds like a line of kings will be from the tribe of Judah. But the sequence of kings will stop when one specific person comes. Then all nations shall obey him.

You are understanding this correctly and it will come to be this way.

But this future is not for the Israelites alone, right? To Abraham you said, "Through your offspring all nations on earth will be blessed, because you have obeyed me."[134] At some point, You will become God for all people, not just these Israelites.

Also true, Moses.

What can You tell me about these things? What more can I see into the future?

These things are indeed things to come but they are not for you to see as yet. The secret things belong to [Me] but the things revealed belong to [you] and to [your] children forever, that [you] may follow all the words of this law.[135]

Moses, I knew from the beginning, from before Adam and Eve, that in giving human beings free will that they would eventually sin against Me and break that relationship. Before you, I worked with many individuals who had faith in Me and with you, I have become the God of this whole nation. I have given you a means through sacrifices of keeping the relationship with Me but part of My secret things is how I plan to work this for all people and all nations. That is beyond your need to know.

It's likely more than I could comprehend. Such knowledge is too wonderful for me, too lofty for me to attain.[136]

Death

Moses has completed the mission that God gave him as he nears the time of his death. He is disappointed that he will not lead the Israelites into the promised land because of his disobedience when he struck the rock rather than speaking to it to provide water. God has also informed him that he will die soon.

Moses: You have told me that my death is soon. Before I die, Let me go over and see the good land beyond the Jordan-that fine hill country and Lebanon.[137] I've come this far in leading Your people. We've waited a long time.

Moses, you know that I will not do that. You must bear the consequences of your sin like others have. And that is enough…do not speak to me anymore about this matter.[138] You cannot enter the land but you can see it. I will show you what I have promised. It is a preview for you to see that My promises are true. This is a great land for them to take over. When you climb the mountain, you will see the land that I promised to Abraham, Isaac, Jacob and to these people.

You know that I am disappointed that I cannot lead them there but I do accept your judgment. In getting things in order, I would first like to talk about my successor. I am pleased that You have selected Joshua. He has been a good and faithful aide all these years. I have commissioned him and encouraged him. I told him, "The Lord himself goes before you and will be with you; he will never leave you nor forsake you. Do not be afraid; do not be discouraged."[139] I know that You will lead him and support him like You did for me.

I will tell him, "As I was with Moses, so I will be with you; I will never leave you nor forsake you. Be strong and courageous."[140] I will continue to encourage him as he moves through the land.

I said after the golden calf incident, do not send us if You will not go with us. It is the same here and I know then that You will continue to go with Your people. I have exhorted them to obey You and choose life. I don't think I can do anything more for them. They are in Your hands and the hands of Joshua.

Moses, I say to Israel, "Do not fear, for I am with you; do not be dismayed, for I am your God. I will strengthen you and help you; I will uphold you with my righteous right hand."[141]

You know, Lord, I really love these people. I had no one for so long and wanted to be accepted by them way back when I was in Egypt but that was not to be. They didn't care much for me when I came back except that You spoke for me. But over these last forty years, I know they have accepted me and they are mine and I am part of them. I am so grateful that you will care for them and continue to love them and fulfill Your promises to them. I could ask nothing more for them.

Lord, my times are in your hands[142] and I know the time for my departure is near. I have fought the good fight, I have finished the race, I have kept the faith.[143]

So, Moses, what do you think about the life you have had?

What a question! I don't want to say much about the first eighty years but I know now that it was a time of preparation for me. The first few years in the desert were hard also but I feel so grateful to You for choosing me. I was so wrong to resist way back then. I would have missed out on so much. You are a sun and shield; [You] bestow favor and honor; no good thing [do You] withhold from those whose walk is blameless. Lord Almighty, blessed is the one who trusts in you.[144] My life would have been so empty if You were not near.

As one nears death, it is natural to wonder if life had purpose, if I accomplished anything worthwhile. And ultimately, it isn't about the things we've accumulated. For a person may labor with wisdom, knowledge and skill, and then they must leave all they own to another who has not toiled for it.[145] You know here in the desert we haven't accumulated anything. I had nothing when I left Egypt. I had nothing when I returned. I leave nothing behind. I know too that whoever loves money never has enough; whoever loves wealth is never satisfied with their income.[146]

So then, if life is not about accumulating things, it must be about intangibles. Did my life have purpose; did I accomplish anything worthwhile? You, Lord, called me into the worthwhile and purposeful aspects of my life. I know that since I wrote these books that others will read and that I've completed the task of bringing Your people here, that I will have a place in history. You will accomplish Your plans and Your plans point to future times. So I do have a legacy and I am honored by You for that. But, Lord, You know that I am not driven by being important. I would wish to just be a humble servant used by You, not someone discussed along with the towering figures of Abraham, Isaac and Jacob.

Moses, you know that they were not driven by self-importance or ego either. They wanted to be obedient to Me.

Lord, I look at the accomplishments I had in Egypt. At the time, they were very important to me and especially so when I was in Midian and did nothing of consequence there. Then, I could point to my education or military actions and other accomplishments with a certain sense of pride. If my life had ended in Midian before You called me, I don't think I would have had much to look back upon as having any impact at all. Yes, I helped Jethro and married and had kids there but was my life really important. I think not. I realized a long time ago that the time in Egypt was only a training ground for me and that what I learned in Egypt was not for self-praise but to prepare me for my future. I see that all that really amounted to very little compared to what You have led me to do.

So, now looking back, did my life make a difference? It did so only because You called me, You went with me, You guided me and You were close to me. I had close loving relations with You and the Israelites as a result and all the relationships were the most important aspects of these last forty years. I know my life made a difference. It was worthwhile and I did accomplish an important task but it is only because of You that is was so.

Moses, well done, good and faithful servant![147]

Thank You, Lord. I learned firsthand from You that You do care for us. We left Egypt and headed into the desert. We hadn't planned on any long term provisions. We relied on You to provide us food and water. During the forty years that [You] led [us] through the wilderness, [our] clothes did not wear out, nor did the sandals on [our] feet.[148] You watched over us and protected us. What could be better than to be in Your presence? I have been privileged to be Your servant. I have been blessed that You speak to me as a friend. Blessed is the people whose God is the Lord.[149]

I have also seen many people die these last forty years. The entire generation, over one million Israelites, who opposed You at Kadesh Barnea have died. I have outlived so many. Aaron, Miriam, even my two sons Gershom and Eliezer have died. I miss those who have passed before me.

Moses, I introduced Myself to you at the burning bush "I am the God of Abraham, the God of Isaac, and the God of Jacob. [I am] not the God of the dead but of the living.[150]

That I know and have discovered in talking with You. I know there is life with You after death. With Your inspiration, I wrote about Enoch who lived long ago. Enoch walked faithfully with God; then he was no more, because God took him away.[151] For all the others, I wrote "and then he died" but not so with Enoch. What a wonderful way to go!

Moses, I am with you also. I will lead you up the mountain and although no one will go with us, My grace is sufficient for you.[152]

No one has come back from death to tell us what it is like. This is unknown for us. We see birth, we see life, we see pain and suffering, we see joy, we see sorrow, we see the sorrow that comes from losing someone we love depart in death, and we can even see them as they experience dying but we cannot see what is on the other side.

Moses, I am on the other side as well as on the side of the living.

So we cannot know what is on the other side except to know You.

Moses, as you have come to know Me, you should also come to know what to expect on the other side. What no eye has seen, what no ear has heard, and what no human mind has conceived— the things [I] have prepared for those who love [Me].[153] My...house has many rooms...[there is] a place for you?[154]

Lord, I can think of some pretty wonderful things and You say what You have prepared is far greater than what I can even think of. I know You are loving and good so what You have prepared is going to be loving and good. I guess it's the process of dying that is so uncertain. I'd like to go like Enoch.

Moses, as we have discussed, life and death are My decisions.

What happens to the people who don't know You when they die? What about those in Canaan who don't know You?

Moses, I am gracious. There are those who have not heard about Me and those who have but have rejected Me. Even if one has not heard specifically about Me, what may be known about [Me] is plain to them, because [I] have made it plain to them. For since the creation of the world [My] invisible qualities—[My] eternal power and divine nature—have been clearly seen, being understood from what has been made, so that people are without excuse.[155] For those whose hearts and minds are open, they can see Me. My grace is sufficient for them.

And those who have heard but reject You?

Moses, I have provided you My commands. You know that those who sin against Me have broken that relationship. They cannot be forgiven without repentance and sacrifice. If one has heard and rejected, they will be eternally separated from Me.

Lord, I am amazed that there are some here who saw You every day in the pillar of cloud or fire and still rejected You. Some have known You but have fallen away.

My righteous one will live by faith. And I take no pleasure in the one who shrinks back. But [you] do not belong to those who shrink back and are destroyed, but to those who have faith and are saved.[156]

Some think there is nothing following death at all. They think this is all there is.

They will be surprised. People are destined to die once, and after that to face judgment.[157] Without a right relationship with Me, they will be separated from Me for eternity.

Lord, there are some who claim to know You but believe in other gods as well or don't accept all You say.

Then they do not know Me. If they knew Me, they would believe what I say. Suppose when you lived in Midian a person told you that he knew your brother Aaron. Suppose he said he knew Aaron was the son of Amram and Jochebed and he had a sister Miriam. You would believe that he did know Aaron. But suppose he said Aaron died at age thirty. You know that to be false and although this person insisted he knew Aaron, you know that your brother is not the person he is describing. So it is with Me. Some may know many things about Me but if they do not believe all about Me that I have revealed, they do not know Me.

When you told the Israelites that they must choose between obedience and rebellion, between life and death, blessings and curses,[158] you told them to choose life. There was no third choice. When I say there are no other gods, how could they know Me and still believe that there are other gods? There is no option for partial rebellion, for partial death, for partial curses. Do I take any pleasure in the death of the wicked? Rather, am I not pleased when they turn from their ways and live?[159] Unless they repent and are forgiven, they will spend eternity separated from Me.

So where do they exist for eternity?

That is not for you to know. All you need to know is that for you and those who are in the right relationship with Me, they will spend eternity with Me.

Some are afraid of what others might think of them or what some may do to them if they showed they loved You.

Do not be afraid of those who kill the body but cannot kill the soul. Rather, be afraid of the One who can destroy both soul and body in hell.[160]

Lord, I am anticipating that I will see faithful friends when I cross over. I miss them.

Moses, you are surrounded by such a great cloud of witnesses,[161] all those of faith who have preceded you.

Lord I am ready. Sovereign Lord…now dismiss your servant in peace.[162]

MOSES: FRIEND OF GOD

Moses: Concluding Thoughts

T he previous chapters have focused on Moses in his time about 3,500 years ago, about 1,500 years before the birth of Jesus. We have the privilege of living in the New Testament era. We have the reality of much of what Moses saw dimly in his prophesy. But why is Moses such a revered person today—so many years later? We know that the larger-than-life portrayals of him are not the real Moses. He was a man that had his flaws but God chose him, called him, molded him, worked with him, provided him the resources to do what He wanted and Moses was obedient. Does obedience alone get one a place in history like Moses? No. As we saw earlier, God expects everyone to be obedient to His leading and, like Moses, when God calls us; he provides the support and resources.

So then, what can we say about Moses that makes him so important to us?

Charles Swindoll says,

> Moses became God's man for a transitional epoch in history. When the divine call came to assume a crucial role in the destiny of men and nations, Moses stepped into the gap. He may have been reluctant. He may have been frightened. He may have been filled with regret and self-doubt. But in the end, he yielded…and became God's instrument in his own generation.[1]

> Consider what he gave up and what he received in return. There was no monument to this man of selfless dedication. No towering sphinx. No imposing pyramid. Egypt was more than willing to forget that such a man ever existed. He was buried on some lonely peak on the barren slopes of Mount Pisgah, without so much as a single flower on his grave.

He willingly traded the earthly monuments and acclaim, the perks, the power, and the pleasure for a reward in an invisible realm. He cashed it all in— every shekel of it—for a relationship with the living God.

It was the best trade anyone could have made. What he lost, he couldn't have kept anyway, and what he gained, he could never lose.[2]

Jonathan Kirsch notes:

Devout tradition in both Judaism and Christianity has always felt obliged to portray Moses as unfailingly good and meek, dignified and devout, righteous and heroic.[3]

And quoting from Moses' last message: This day I call the heavens and the earth as witnesses against you that I have set before you life and death, blessings and curses. Now choose life, so that you and your children may live and that you may love the Lord your God, listen to his voice, and hold fast to him. For the Lord is your life, and he will give you many years in the land he swore to give to your fathers, Abraham, Isaac and Jacob[4], Kirsch says,

No matter how we conceive of Moses, no matter how we remember him, he insists on confronting us with tough choices—love or hate, hope or despair, compassion or cruelty—and he insists, too, that we must choose for ourselves. And so the last word on Moses, and our urgent prayer, ought to be: May we choose wisely and well.[5]

The biblical account of Moses and his writing in the first five books of the Bible reflects both his character in humility and God's authorship in that Moses is not presented as "an unfailingly good and meek, dignified and devout, righteous and heroic," as Kirsch suggests.

As so many of God's selected leaders, Moses was a real person. He was not perfect. He wasn't groomed for the task to be assigned. God called him when he was least expecting it. He had his own baggage and failings. However, by the end of his life, he was greatly revered by his people. God saw Moses's heart and knew that He could use him. God led him into the role he would play. Moses obediently followed and his reputation and accomplishments are remembered these 3,500 years later.

Moses· God's Plan

The life of Moses reveals God's hand in all the circumstances from his birth to final meeting with God and his death. His life was as miraculous as the burning bush. He never should have survived after his birth. How could his mother have been so inspired to place him in a basket in the river? How could he have been in just the right place for Pharaoh's daughter to find him? What would draw the Egyptian woman to want to care for a slave child? How could his Egyptian mother have defied the Pharaoh to bring him into the palace? How could he have survived when Pharaoh knew of his treachery? How could he have gained an audience so frequently with the Pharaoh?

The only answer to these questions is that God wanted it that way. How perfectly God orchestrated the rivers of time! Moses had to have an education that included writing so that God could provide for us the inspired writings of the first five books of the Bible. Had someone come along prior to Moses to lead the people it is likely they would not have known how to write because writing in this form had not yet been developed nor would the person have had the education necessary.

Had someone tried to lead the Israelites out of slavery earlier, they likely would have been too small a nation to be able to defeat the inhabitants of the land they had been promised. Had someone come later, the Israelite nation would likely have been too large to be able to sustain through the wanderings in the desert. The Pharaohs were already concerned over the size of the nations and more drastic measures to reduce that threat may have been undertaken.

Moses's call and return to Egypt was also perfectly timed. Not only did Moses have time to be humbled and prepared but God prepared the Egyptian leadership to receive him.

The failure of the Israelites to seize the first opportunity to take the promised land was certainly not a surprise to God. It proved an important lesson in obedience to the Israelites but the extra thirty-eight years in wandering provided the opportunity to grow from a slave mentality to a chosen race mentality. The time certainly was not wasted because they learned military tactics and learned to read and write. In Moses's final message, he tells the Israelites to keep God commandments and to write them on the doorframes of your houses and on your gates.[6]

If he were to go through his life history, Moses could point to many times when God's hand was on him to guide him. It is the same for many of us, if our eyes are open and we can see. God looks on the heart for people who are willing to be obedient, not because they are perfect.

Moses· Legacy

Moses is mentioned many times in the succeeding books of the Bible. Most of the time, it is in relation to the giving of the law or by reference to the law itself but he is also commended for his faith and leadership.

The Pharisees claimed, "We are disciples of Moses!"[7] Discipleship means much more that being a follower. A disciple is a person who is a student or adherent of the doctrines of another but even more, seeks to put into action the teachings of the person followed. The Pharisees saw Moses as one they desired to follow completely and to obey his teaching. However, Jesus calls them on this failure when He said, "Your accuser is Moses, on whom your hopes are set. If you believed Moses, you would believe me, for he wrote about me."[8]

In the transfiguration, Moses appears to Peter, James and John along with Elijah[9] speaking with Jesus. Moses appearing in glory here speaks of his importance.

Moses· Obedience

Moses's life shows us an example for Christians today. How can that be since for Moses, Jesus birth was still about 1,500 years into the future?

Jesus calls to us: "Whoever wants to be my disciple must deny themselves and take up their cross and follow me. For whoever wants to save their life will lose it, but whoever loses their life for me and for the gospel will save it."[10]

In 2016, my son Andrew, as Lead Pastor at Branches HB, Huntington Beach, California, taught a series entitled "Come and Die." This is not an especially inviting title in an age where many Christian churches are promoting self-gratification and watered-down, feel-good Christianity. Today, many are tempted to repeat words of Isaiah:

> They say to the seers, "See no more visions!" and
> to the prophets, "Give us no more visions of what
> is right! Tell us pleasant things, prophesy illusions.
> Leave this way, get off this path, and stop confronting
> us with the Holy One of Israel!"[11]

However, Jesus's call is one of true discipleship. We are called to be confronted with the truths of discipleship including the denying of self and taking up the cross. There is a cost to this discipleship and death to ourselves that is necessary in order for disciples of Jesus to experience the true life that is found on the other side of the cross for any who are willing to follow him.

This may not be a pleasant task and certainly was not one for Moses. It was hard. He called out to God in his hardship but we can see Moses in Jesus's call. He certainly denied himself and his life, accepted God's call and through obedience, carried out his responsibilities. In a real sense, he lost his old life and in so doing, gained life. As I have searched in the Bible, only Abraham and Moses have been noted to be God's friend. (Certainly, others walked with God and David was a man after God's own heart. Later, Jesus identified his disciples as friends.)

From the time that Moses accepted his calling to lead the Israelites, he was obedient to God (except for the one time that he failed in frustration—a real human thing to do). Moses is not afraid to detail his own failing and this leads to greater credibility in his telling of the story. Obedience was one of the topics I suspect he discussed directly with God and we discussed in the chapter "The Wandering in the Desert".

We discussed Moses as being obedient but that alone would not be sufficient to be called friend nor would it lead so many to revere him today.

Moses· Humility

One of the qualities we admire in others is humility. It's hard to be friends with an arrogant, prideful, or conceited person. The arrogant cannot stand in your presence. You hate all who do wrong; you destroy those who tell lies, the bloodthirsty and deceitful you, Lord, detest.[12] He (God) mocks proud mockers but shows favor to the humble and oppressed.[13]

The Bible is full of admiration for a person who truly demonstrates humility. False humility is not desirable but true humility in recognizing the value of others and not elevating oneself above them is honored. Humble yourselves before the Lord, and he will lift you up.[14]

Moses may not have started out as a humble person but by the time he was called by God, he had developed humility. Described later as a very humble man, more humble than anyone else on the face of the earth,[15] I suspect God saw that possibility in his character and with some time in humble surroundings could be used by God in carrying out His plans.

Andrew also spoke to this in the "Come and Die" series. Living sacrificially as disciples of Jesus includes laying down our rights and self-interest, and valuing others over ourselves for the sake of being united in Christ. Only by giving preferential treatment to others and holding others above ourselves can one begin to take on the humility of Jesus, who, being fully God, laid down the power and glory that were rightfully His to make Himself nothing; a servant who was even obedient to death on a cross.

While Moses was humble and obedient, I think God saw another character trait in Moses that led to their friendship.

Moses· Love

I think the greatest quality that God saw in Moses when He called him was his capacity for love. Moses did not have much opportunity to demonstrate this love for others until God's call although he did show concern for his people in his failed attempt at rebellion against Pharaoh. However, it didn't take long after being called that Moses did exhibit that love for others. He stood in the gap for his fellow Israelites in interceding for them with God. He led them, he judged rightly and fairly, he showed them God's favor. He was concerned over their welfare. He led them and urged them in the right path.

Again in the "Come and Die" series, Andrew taught on love, explaining how all the actions we are called into as disciples are centered around love and how God's love is the foundation for the kind of community He wants us to be: selfless and concerned with the interests of others, holding them higher than ourselves. For Jesus's disciples' faith, hope, and love are paramount but when we pass into eternity and all things are revealed, the only practice that has any use or relevance in heaven, and the greatest of all will be love.[16]

Therefore, I think the qualities Moses possessed that were so pleasing to God that he was His friend were obedience, humility and love. Why is love so important?

God Is Love

One may argue with my logic in understanding the conversations between God and Moses or may differ with my conclusions. Certainly, that is possible and I don't think my responses are exhaustive of the conversations that could have occurred. As I said before, I claim no new revelations on God's Word and that Word is available to all of us. However, I would challenge anyone who studies the first five books of the Bible to see God as anything other than loving. Throughout this history and interactions with His creation, God has been gracious and loving. At the same time, God is just and holy. He requires holiness on the part of His people and He will administer justice in accordance with His character. Humankind, on the other hand, vacillates between acceptance, partial acceptance and rejection. Many like to see the loving characteristic of God but prefer not to face the holy and just characteristics.

His plans as revealed through Moses also lead to the conclusion that since the beginning of time, God had a plan for us that lead to Jesus and His sacrificial death for us and in His resurrection, a promise of eternal life for all who believe. The giving of the Law and atonement for sins through sacrifice was not a plan B after the failure in the garden of Eden any more than Jesus's death and resurrection a plan C after the failures of the Israelites under the Law. God says from the beginning that there is one plan and that was for Jesus to come and take our substitutionary death in order for us to have this right relationship with Him. That is His desire. This is why we were created. He delights in His people when they are in a right relationship with Him.

Search the Bible for the word *love* and you will find so many references. The Bible is God's message of love to us all. The Apostle John is so good as describing God's love. In fact, he says, God is love[17] and love comes from God.[18] When we truly love someone, it can only occur because of God whether we recognize it or not. We cannot truly love someone unless God is with us. No one has ever seen God; but if we love one another, God lives in us and his love is made complete in us…If anyone acknowledges that Jesus is the Son of God, God lives in them and they in God.[19] And there it is. For God so loved the world that he gave his one and only Son, that whoever believes in him shall not perish but have eternal life.[20] That was God's plan from the beginning. Jesus is the fulfillment of the promise to Abraham all peoples on earth will be blessed through you[21]. Jesus said, I am the way and the truth and the life. No one comes to the Father except through me.[22] Therefore, since Jesus was God's plan for our salvation from the beginning, it is not possible to go to the Father, God, without Jesus. Just as we discussed in the chapter Glimpse Ahead, anyone who professes to believe in God without Jesus is talking about someone other than the God of the Bible, the God of creation, the God who loves us, the God who is Love. But the good news is that God wants all people to be saved and to come to a knowledge of the truth. For there is one God and one mediator between God and mankind, the man Christ Jesus, who gave himself as a ransom for all people.[23]

This is love; not that we loved God, but that he loved us and send his Son as an atoning sacrifice for our sins.[24]

John continues to say, Dear friends, since God so loved us, we also ought to love one another.[25] So as followers of Jesus Christ in discipleship, how do we show this love for others?

A Handy Little Gadget

When we think of love and demonstrating love for others, we often think of giving gifts. When my oldest son, Michael, was in elementary school, the teachers created a gift store at Christmas where the students could buy gifts for others. Michael bought me a combination screwdriver with an insert that was a flat blade on one end or Phillips head on the other. The thing that made this memorable was that after thanking him for the gift, he said, "It looked like a handy little gadget."

We know that God the Father loves Jesus, His Son[26] and that the Son loves the Father.[27] I wondered how they may show their love for each other through the giving of gifts. How does one give a gift to someone who truly has it all?

As Jesus prays for His disciples, He says, "I have revealed you (the Father) to those whom you gave me out of the world. They were yours; you gave them to me."[28] Later in that same prayer, Jesus includes "I pray also for those who will believe in me through their message."[29] Therefore, Jesus describes believers as a gift from the Father. How could believers be a gift? What possible value does a believer bring to Jesus?

Jesus says, "Glory has come to me through them."[30] So collectively, believers bring Him glory but with all the glory that Jesus possesses, of what value is one believer? Jesus says, "I protected them and kept them safe by the name you gave me. None has been lost except the one doomed to destruction so that Scripture would be fulfilled."[31] Thus, every believer is cherished by Jesus. He accepts the gift of each believer that is given by the Father and this brings Jesus glory.

Through His obedience and death, Jesus provided the means for believers to come to the Father. Thus, each believer is a gift to the Father. What value does each believer have for the Father? Sing to the Lord a new song, his praise from the ends of the earth…let them give glory to the Lord and proclaim his praise.[32] The believer brings additional glory to the Father. Considering how glorious is the Father, can He value each believer? In the parable of the lost son, the Father sees his returning son a long way off and he ran to his son, threw his arms around him and kissed him.[33] The Father says, for this son of mine was dead and is alive again; he was lost and is found.[34] And as we previously discovered, there is rejoicing in the presence of the angels of God over one sinner who repents.[35] So, yes God is pleased with the gift from the Son of the believer. He receives praise and glory and each gift is cherished.

Therefore, since the believer is the Father's love gift to the Son and the believer is the Son's love gift to the Father, how can we not see the value in each other as They do? How do we show and acknowledge this value except through love?

What does this mean practically? Love is patient, love is kind. It does not envy, it does not boast, it is not proud. It does not dishonor others, it is not self-seeking, it is not easily angered, it keeps no record of wrongs. Love does not delight in evil but rejoices with the truth. It always protects, always trusts, always hopes, always perseveres. Love never fails.[36]

This is how we are to respond to each other because of the indescribable gift the Father has lavished on us. And since this is to be part of our character, it ought to be our character regardless of the response of people to us. It isn't meant only for fellow Christians but for all. But this again is hard. It is not in our normal character to do this.

I found myself waiting behind another car at an intersection, both of us signaling a right turn. The light was red but there were no approaching cars and I wondered why this person of obvious low intelligence was not turning. Then I saw the pedestrian approach the curb. I realized that I was impatient. But I didn't want to be. Because I wanted and prayed to be more patient, that situation stays with me and I am doing better. I haven't perfected any of these acts of love. We are not able on our own to change into this love character. We are not always patient; we are not always kind, etc. As Andrew taught in the "Come and Die" series, the reality is that every follower of Jesus needs to be lead by Christ from within; we need Him to live through us, moment to moment as the Spirit of God works in our hearts and minds to see real change happen in us.

Then, possessing humility, obedience, and love, perhaps we can be prepared like Moses in the hands of the Father to be His "handy little gadget" as a tool to accomplish His purposes.

EPILOGUE

Further Questions

I have supposed questions and concerns that Moses may have had at his time that are relevant to our own times. Today, people still have questions about God's nature, who we are, what is God doing, why bad things happen to good people, etc. I have had these questions and others, in friendly conversations have had them also. As I read in Exodus that God spoke to Moses as a friend, it became the motivation to write this book. We all have questions and it is healthy to ask them.

I have not attempted to thoroughly discuss all the possible responses. I have not attempted to discuss the very personal issues that Moses may have discussed relating to his relationships with Zipporah, sons, and others and very personal questions we may have related to family discord, suicide, drug abuse, etc. However, my purpose is not to answer all questions but to point to where the answers may be found.

Many of us have the Bible close at hand but do not read and study it. When my daughter Shelly was in high school, her youth director sponsored a trip to the Soviet Union shortly before its demise. She recalls giving a Russian language Bible to some young Russian boys who cried at the experience of holding and having a Bible. I would encourage the reader to pick up the Bible that is close at hand and establish a habit of daily reading.

I confess that I have not always been a daily Bible reader. It took the encouragement of others and the calling of the Holy Spirit that started me and sustained me. I found that I needed a set time and place to make this a daily habit.

This has changed for me as well from an evening reading to the morning. I gain new insights each time I read through even very familiar passages as the Spirit reveals new truths. I miss the times I failed to spend time alone with God in His Word.

I suspect that for each of us as we seek God's responses in the Bible, the personal nature of our questions will lead us as He directs. There may be questions for which the answer is simply "Trust God."

The most significant difference between the questions Moses may have had and what we have is that we are on the other side of the cross. Moses's relationship was based upon the law and sacrifices. While he was unable to keep the law perfectly, sacrifices provided the means of grace to forgiveness and restoration of the relationship with the Father. For us, Jesus is the perfect Lamb of God, without blemish. We have been made holy through the sacrifice of the body of Jesus Christ once for all.[1] Through Christ, we have been restored in our relationship with the Father and can have this personal relationship. I believe that the Bible has answers today for most of these questions. Perhaps as I have done, the reader starts with the question and searches the Scriptures for answers. It is better that in the daily reading of the Bible, scripture comes alive so that God is always answering our questions through the inspiration of the Holy Spirit. I suggest there will be questions for which we will need to wait until we see God face-to-face to understand His answers. By then in His presence though, the questions will appear irrelevant. For now, we will need to rely in faith that God is all knowing, all good, all loving, always present and always faithful for those who love Him and are in the right relationship with Him through the gracious sacrificial death and resurrection of His Son, Jesus Christ.

ENDNOTES

Preface

1 Exodus 33:11
² 2 Timothy 3:16

Introduction

¹ Exodus 34:29
² Exodus 17:14

Chapter 1 First Forty Years

¹ Exodus 1:7
² Exodus 12:37
³ Exodus 12:37
⁴ Op cit. Davis, p.154
⁵ Exodus 1:10
⁶ Exodus 1:13
⁷ Exodus 1:16
⁸ Op. Cit. Davis, p.62
⁹ Exodus 2:10
¹⁰ Acts 7:22
¹¹ Op.cit. Davis, p.40
¹² Ibid., p. 42
¹³ Thutmose III The Napoleon of Ancient Egypt 1479 – 1425 BC, http://discoveringegypt.com/ancient-egyptian-kings-queens/thutmose-iii-thenapoleon-of-ancient-egypt/ [accessed 11/27/15]
¹⁴ *Ancient Egypt, An Overview*, http://history-world.org/ancient_egypt. htm [accessed 12/7/15]
¹⁵ Acts 7:23
¹⁶ Op.cit. Davis, p. 64.
¹⁷ Op. cit. Swindoll, p. 39
¹⁸ R. A. Guisepi, *Writing*, The International History Project, 1999, http://history-world.org/writing.htm [accessed 11/25/15]

[19] *Ancient Egypt, An Overview*, http://history-world.org/ancient_egypt. htm. Accessed on December 8, 2015.

[20] Ibid.

[21] ibid

[22] *History of Astronomy*, University of Oregon, http://abyss.uoregon. edu/~js/ ast121/lectures/lec02.html. Accessed on December 8, 2015.

[23] Egyptian Astronomy, Martyn Shuttleworth, https://explorable.com/ egyptian-astronomy?gid=1595. Accessed on July 8, 2016.

[24] *History of Mathematics*, http://www.historyworld.net/wrldhis/PlainText Histories.asp?historyid=aa50. Accessed December 8, 2015.

[25] *Egyptian Pyramids*, http://www.history.com/topics/ancient-history/ theegyptian-pyramids. Accessed on December 10, 2015.

[26] How Pyramids Work, http://science.howstuffworks.com/engineering/ structural/pyramid3.htm. Accessed December 10, 2015.

[27] Joshua 5:4,5

[28] Exodus 3:7,8

[29] Exodus 1:15

Chapter 2 Second Forty Years

[1] Hebrews 11:24,25
[2] Acts 7:23
[3] Exodus 2:11
[4] Acts 7:25
[5] Exodus 3:1
[6] Genesis 46:34
[7] Genesis 30:43
[8] Exodus 4:24-26
[9] Exodus 2:1
[10] Exodus 2:4
[11] Exodus 7:7
[12] Exodus 2:22
[13] Exodus 18:4, I Chronicles 12:15
[14] Numbers 12:1
[15] Moses Ethiopian Wife, Bible Study Monthly, http://www.biblefellowshi-punion.co.uk/2004/sep_oct/moseseth.htm. Accessed on August 19, 2016.
[16] Exodus 3:4
[17] Exodus 3:6
[18] Exodus 18:4
[19] Exodus 3:10
[20] Exodus 18:11
[21] Exodus 4:24
[22] Exodus 18:2–5

Chapter 3 Between Egypt and Canaan

1. Exodus 7:1
2. Exodus 5:1
3. Exodus 6:1
4. Exodus 14:31
5. Exodus 19:5
6. Numbers 14:22,23
7. Genesis 15:5,6
8. Genesis 15:18
9. Genesis 17:7
10. Genesis 26:2–5
11. Genesis 28:13–15
12. Genesis 17:10,11
13. Genesis 17:23
14. Joshua 5:4,5
15. Davis, op. cit., p.169
16. Egyptian Religion, Peter F. Dorman, Encyclopaedia Britannica, http:// www. britannica.com/topic/Egyptian-religion#ref559385. Accessed on December 7, 2015.
17. Sumerian Religion, http://www.crystalinks.com/sumereligion.html. Accessed on December 7, 2015.
18. Genesis 31:19
19. Genesis 25:2
20. What is the religion of the Midian people?, http://christianity.stackexchange. com/questions/15372/what-is-the-religion-of-the-midian-people.   Accessed on December 8, 2015.
21. Numbers 22
22. Isaiah 44:6
23. Exodus 20:3
24. Psalm 115:4–8
25. 1 Timothy 6:17
26. Luke 6:24–26
27. Isaiah 42:8
28. Exodus 20:5,6
29. Romans 2:5
30. 1 Timothy 2:4
31. Ezra 33:11
32. Matthew 13:15,16
33. Matthew 7:7,8
34. John 3:20
35. 2 Corinthians 7:10
36. Hebrews 4:2
37. Romans 10:17

38 Hebrews 9:19
39 1 John 1:3
40 Exodus 4:12
41 Exodus 15:6,7
42 Deuteronomy 32:4
43 Psalm 25:8–10
44 1 John 4:8
45 Exodus 10:3
46 Isaiah 40:31
47 Exodus 3:7
48 Hebrews 13:5
49 Habakkuk 2:4
50 Hebrews 11:1
51 Hebrews 11:8–10
52 Genesis 15:5
53 Romans 4:18–20
54 Genesis 15:6
55 Romans 10:17
56 Romans 2:6
57 Matthew 5:45
58 Philippians 4:6
59 Isaiah 41:10
60 Romans 1:18
61 Psalm 19:1
62 Matthew 19:17
63 Exodus 20:15
64 Romans 3:23
65 Deuteronomy 18:10
66 Isaiah 43:10
67 Isaiah 55:5
68 Exodus 3:11
69 Genesis 18:11
70 Matthew 19:26
71 1 Samuel 16:7
72 1 Timothy 1:13
73 2 Corinthians 12:9
74 Galatians 3:6
75 Matthew 9:36
76 Exodus 4:11, 12
77 2 Kings 19:25
78 Psalm 127:1
79 John 15:5
80 Psalm 139:13–16
81 Isaiah 14:24

82 Genesis 15:16
83 Psalm 65:4
84 Psalm 139:23,24
85 2 Chronicles 1:10
86 Exodus 33:12
87 Exodus 33:14
88 Exodus 33:16
89 Exodus 33:17
90 Deuteronomy 31:8
91 Isaiah 40:31
92 Exodus 3:8
93 Genesis 17:6,7
94 Deuteronomy 4:34
95 Exodus 6: 2,3
96 Exodus 3:6
97 Ibid.
98 Exodus 7:4,5
99 Proverbs 9:10
100 Exodus 9:16
101 Exodus 6:8
102 Exodus 6:6
103 Jeremiah 29:11
104 Deuteronomy 2:25
105 Deuteronomy 4:6–8
106 Genesis 22:18
107 Exodus 19:5,6
108 Psalm 145:13
109 Exodus 32:1
110 Deuteronomy 4:4
111 Deuteronomy 4:10
112 Exodus 20:3,4
113 Exodus 32:4,5
114 Isaiah 44:13–19
115 Jeremiah 10:5
116 Isaiah 58:11
117 Deuteronomy 6:5
118 Deuteronomy 12:31
119 Exodus 34:15
120 Isaiah 5:20,21
121 Isaiah 55:8
122 John 4:24
123 Deuteronomy 4:15–19
124 Exodus 14:12
125 Exodus 34:8,9

[126] Exodus 32:9
[127] Genesis 3:6
[128] Genesis 3:5
[129] 1 Timothy 2:4
[130] James 1:13–15
[131] Hebrews 12:7–11
[132] Deuteronomy 4:40
[133] Deuteronomy 39:9,10
[134] Leviticus 26:3–13
[135] Genesis 1:26,27
[136] Colossians 3:23,24
[137] 1 Corinthians 12:15–20
[138] Ephesians 2:8,9
[139] Matthew 7:7,8
[140] Romans 10:17
[141] Deuteronomy 6:6
[142] John 20:29
[143] Proverbs 1:7
[144] 2 Corinthians 5:7
[145] Romans 10:10
[146] Deuteronomy 31:27, 29
[147] Exodus 34:9
[148] Exodus 19:5
[149] Davis op. cit., p.207
[150] Ibid. p. 209
[151] Matthew 22:37
[152] Exodus 20:7
[153] Leviticus 19:12
[154] Leviticus 22:32
[155] Exodus 20:8,9
[156] Genesis 2:2,3
[157] Deuteronomy 5:14
[158] Isaiah 58:13,14
[159] Exodus 20:12
[160] 1 Timothy 3:4
[161] Proverbs 17:6
[162] Proverbs 23:22–24
[163] Exodus 20:13
[164] Genesis 2:7
[165] Deuteronomy 32:39
[166] Job 29:12
[167] Leviticus 19:16–17
[168] Matthew 5:22
[169] Proverbs 17:5

170 Exodus 20:14
171 Matthew 19:5,6
172 Proverbs 5:1–6
173 Matthew 5:28
174 1 Corinthians 13:4–7
175 Proverbs 5:15–18
176 Exodus 20:15
177 Proverbs 14:23
178 Psalm 104:27,28
179 Matthew 6:3,4
180 Ecclesiastes 5:10
181 Leviticus 19:13
182 Philippians 2:3,4
183 Exodus 20:16
184 Leviticus 19:16
185 Exodus 23:1
186 Leviticus 19:15
187 Exodus 23:2
188 Exodus 23: 6,8
189 1 Thessalonians 5:11,14
190 Ephesians 4:25, 29–32
191 Exodus 20:17
192 Proverbs 14:30
193 1 Timothy 6:6
194 Luke 12:15
195 Proverbs 27:20
196 Philippians 4:6–7
197 Isaiah 58:9–11
198 Colossians 3:5,8,9,12–14
199 Colossians 3:2
200 Philippians 4:8
201 Exodus 20:19
202 Leviticus 20:26
203 Leviticus 18:3,4
204 Exodus 12:14
205 Exodus 12:42
206 Exodus 28:1
207 Leviticus 11:47
208 Genesis 3:8
209 Leviticus 4:27, 28, 35
210 Leviticus 6:2–5,7
211 Leviticus 1:9
212 Leviticus 2:8,9
213 Leviticus 3:16

[214] Hebrews 10:22
[215] Genesis 12:12, 20:2
[216] Genesis 2:18
[217] Genesis 2:24
[218] Matthew 19:6
[219] Proverbs 5:18
[220] Psalm 139:13
[221] Isaiah 14:24
[222] Exodus 20:16
[223] Leviticus 18:3
[224] 1 Corinthians 6:18
[225] Mark 12:30,31
[226] Genesis 3:6
[227] 1 Corinthians 10:13
[228] Genesis 9:1
[229] 1 Corinthians 13:4–8
[230] Leviticus 11:45
[231] Philippians 2:3,4
[232] Mark 10:5
[233] Mark 10:11,12
[234] Matthew 5:48
[235] Leviticus 11:44
[236] Romans 3:23
[237] Romans 3:10
[238] Matthew 22:37
[239] Acts 3:19
[240] Leviticus 2:9
[241] Leviticus 16:8
[242] Leviticus 16:20–22
[243] Hebrews 9:22
[244] Leviticus 26:44
[245] Leviticus 26:3
[246] Leviticus 26:12
[247] Leviticus 26:14
[248] Isaiah 29:13
[249] Habakkuk 1:13

Chapter 4 The Wandering in the Desert

[1] Numbers 21:3
[2] Numbers 21:34
[3] Numbers 20:10
[4] Numbers 20:12
[5] Numbers 26:51

6 Psalm 75:2
7 Isaiah 40:31
8 Proverbs 3:5,6
9 Jeremiah 29:11
10 Proverbs 12:5
11 1 Timothy 6:15
12 Matthew 10:29
13 Job 39:1
14 Job 41:11
15 Galatians 4:4
16 Genesis 15:16
17 2 Peter 3:8
18 1 Corinthians 2:9
19 Psalm 65:4
20 2 Peter 3:9
21 Isaiah 60:22
22 2 Peter 3:9
23 Genesis 27:2
24 Ezekiel 18:32
25 John 10:10
26 Mark 12:30, 31
27 Deuteronomy 6:6–9
28 Zechariah 7:10
29 Isaiah 14:24
30 Genesis 45:5,7
31 Proverbs 3:1–6
32 Romans 12:2
33 Hosea 6:6
34 Matthew 6:7,8
35 Romans 8:28
36 1 Corinthians 13: 4-8
37 Titus 3:14
38 Colossians 3:23
39 Zechariah 7:9,10
40 Exodus 19:8
41 Hebrew 11:7
42 Hebrew 11:8
43 Genesis 15:5
44 Genesis 15:6
45 Romans 6:16
46 Exodus 20:8
47 Numbers 20:8
48 Numbers 20:10
49 Deuteronomy 5:33

50 Luke 17:10

51 Who Built it First? History Website, http://www.history.com/shows/ancient-discoveries/articles/who-built-it-first-2. Accessed on August 2, 2016.

52 A Brief History of the Ancient science of Sword making, Robbie Gonzalez, http://io9.gizmodo.com/5831683/a-brief-history-of-the-ancient-science-of-sword-making. Accessed on August 2, 2016.

53 The History of Archery, http://www.historyoffighting.com/archery.php. Accessed on August 19, 2016.

54 Exodus 13:17

55 Matthew 5:9

56 Romans 12:18

57 1 Samuel 16:7

58 Philippians 2:3,4

59 Proverbs 16:28

60 Proverbs 16:18

61 Matthew 18:15,16

62 Proverbs 29:22

63 Ephesians 5:3

64 Romans 13:1,2

65 Romans 13:4

66 Leviticus 25:53,54

67 Ezekiel 18:32

68 Psalm 8:4

69 John 15:19

70 Proverbs 5:22,23

71 Exodus 23:32,33

72 2 Peter 2:9

73 Matthew 12:35

74 Colossians 3:5

75 Jeremiah 29:13

76 Numbers 16:3

77 Numbers 16:13

78 Jeremiah 23:30, 31

79 Matthew 7:20

80 1 Timothy 2:4

81 Matthew 5:14,16

82 Luke 6:32

83 Matthew 5:44

84 Job 14:1

85 Isaiah 48:22

86 Isaiah 26:3,4

87 *Ptolemaic system*, Alexander Raymong Jones, Encyclopaedia Britannica, http://www.britannica.com/topic/Ptolemaic-system. Accessed on December 08, 2015.

[88] Creation Mythology, Richard Deurer, 2010, http://www.egyptartsite. com/ crea.html. Accessed on February 10, 2016.

[89] Genesis 1:1

[90] Job 25:2

[91] Genesis 1:3

[92] Genesis 1:11

[93] Genesis 1:20

[94] Genesis 2:19

[95] Job 39:20

[96] Job 39:27

[97] Job 39:1

[98] Job 40:15,16

[99] Hebrews 11:1

[100] Genesis 1:27

[101] Genesis 2:7

[102] Genesis 2:18

[103] Genesis 2:21

[104] Genesis 2:22

[105] Genesis 2:24

[106] Genesis 1:31

[107] Psalm 8:3,4

[108] Exodus 35:31,32

[109] Exodus 35:35

[110] Psalm 139:13,15

[111] Psalm 90:4

[112] Genesis 2:1

[113] Exodus 20:8

[114] Genesis 34:2

[115] Romans 3:23

[116] Leviticus 20:2

[117] Genesis 1:30

[118] Genesis 2:15

[119] James 1:13

[120] James 1:14,15

[121] 1 Corinthians 10:13

[122] Deuteronomy 32:4

[123] Romans 5:12

[124] John 16:33

[125] James 2:10

[126] Isaiah 55:8

[127] Romans 9:15

[128] Matthew 10:29,31

[129] Hebrew 9:27

[130] Isaiah 41:13

131 2 Corinthians 1:3
132 Deuteronomy 31:8
133 Deuteronomy 30:19,20

Chapter 5 Glimpse Ahead

1 Genesis 48:16
2 Deuteronomy 2:25
3 Exodus 24:13
4 Genesis 12:7
5 Deuteronomy 11:26
6 Deuteronomy 34:7
7 Deuteronomy 34:10
8 Exodus 4:1
9 Numbers 16:28
10 Romans 13:1
11 Exodus 5:1
12 Exodus 40:38
13 Exodus 33:16
14 Exodus 4:10
15 Exodus 3:17
16 Exodus 3:12
17 Exodus 5:22,23
18 Exodus 10:1,2
19 Exodus 19:5,6
20 Exodus 19:9
21 Exodus 32:10
22 Psalm 106:23
23 Numbers 11:12, 14
24 Numbers 11:17
25 Deuteronomy 31:24
26 Romans 10:17
27 Deuteronomy 9:5
28 Acts 23:1
29 Proverbs 11:2
30 Proverbs 22:4
31 Proverbs 9:10
32 Numbers 12:3
33 Swindoll, p. 339
34 Exodus 34:34, 35
35 Genesis 2:18
36 Ecclesiastes 4:9–11
37 Ecclesiastes 4:12
38 Numbers 20:6

39 Proverbs 12:26
40 Proverbs 22:24, 25
41 Genesis 18:32
42 I Corinthians 15:33
43 Proverbs 17:17
44 Proverbs 9:10
45 Romans 12:9
46 James 3:13
47 Proverbs 27:17
48 1 Timothy 3:2-4
49 James 3:1
50 Exodus 18:21
51 Isaiah 40:31
52 Proverbs 12:15, 16
53 Psalm 119:125
54 Psalm 55:22
55 Mark 6:31
56 Deuteronomy 7:3
57 2 Corinthians 6:14
58 1 Corinthians 7:12, 13
59 Isaiah 5:20
60 Psalm 34:18
61 Deuteronomy 31:8
62 Exodus 3:5
63 Leviticus 11:45
64 Deuteronomy 7:6
65 Deuteronomy 11:25
66 Deuteronomy 11:1
67 Deuteronomy 9:24
68 Exodus 19:5, 6
69 Leviticus 22:32
70 Leviticus 19:2
71 Leviticus 5:17
72 Romans 6:23
73 Deuteronomy 29:20
74 Hebrews 9:22
75 Leviticus 4:32, 33
76 Leviticus 4:35
77 Leviticus 17:11
78 Leviticus 16:34
79 Deuteronomy 17:7
80 Deuteronomy 19:19
81 Deuteronomy 19:13
82 Deuteronomy 17:12

[83] Deuteronomy 21:21
[84] Deuteronomy 24:7
[85] Deuteronomy 22:21
[86] Deuteronomy 13:5
[87] Deuteronomy 13:11
[88] Deuteronomy 26:17–19
[89] Psalm 103:6
[90] Psalm 18:30
[91] Isaiah 25:1
[92] Psalm 149:4
[93] 1 John 4:16
[94] Psalm 147:11
[95] Psalm 37:4
[96] Psalm 9:2
[97] Psalm 98:4
[98] Luke 11:13
[99] Luke 15:10
[100] 1 Corinthians 1:25
[101] 1 Corinthians 1:19
[102] Proverbs 2:6
[103] 2 Corinthians 9:6
[104] 2 Corinthians 9:11
[105] Malachi 4:1
[106] 1 Peter 5:5
[107] Matthew 23:12
[108] Matthew 5:8
[109] Romans 8:28
[110] Genesis 21:6
[111] Mark 10:27
[112] 1 Corinthians 7:7
[113] Numbers 18:6
[114] Exodus 36:1
[115] Colossians 3:23
[116] Leviticus 1:17
[117] 1 Timothy 5:4
[118] Genesis 1:31
[119] Isaiah 40:26
[120] Job 39:1
[121] Job 39:13
[122] Psalm 50:10, 11
[123] Psalm 19:14
[124] Deuteronomy 7:22
[125] Deuteronomy 31:16, 17, 21
[126] Deuteronomy 30:2,3

[127] Deuteronomy 31:26, 29
[128] 2 Timothy 3:16
[129] Psalm 86:5
[130] Deuteronomy 17:15–19
[131] Genesis 3:15
[132] Deuteronomy 18:18,19
[133] Genesis 49:10
[134] Genesis 22:18
[135] Deuteronomy 29:29
[136] Psalm 139:6
[137] Deuteronomy 3:25
[138] Deuteronomy 3:26
[139] Deuteronomy 31:8
[140] Joshua 1:5,6
[141] Isaiah 41:10
[142] Psalm 31:15
[143] 2 Timothy 4:6,7
[144] Psalm 84:11, 12
[145] Ecclesiastes 2:21
[146] Ecclesiastes 5:10
[147] Matthew 25:21
[148] Deuteronomy 29:5
[149] Psalm 144:15
[150] Matthew 22:32
[151] Genesis 5:24
[152] 2 Corinthians 12:9
[153] 1 Corinthians 2:9
[154] John 14:2
[155] Romans 1:19, 20
[156] Hebrews 10:38, 39
[157] Hebrews 9:27
[158] Deuteronomy 30:19
[159] Ezekiel 18:23
[160] Matthew 10:28
[161] Hebrews 12:1
[162] Luke 2:29

Chapter 6 Moses: Friend of God

[1] Swindoll, p.2
[2] Ibid. p. 366
[3] Kirsch, p.2
[4] Deuteronomy 30:19,20
[5] Ibid. p.366

6 Deuteronomy 6:9
7 John 9:28
8 John 5:45, 46
9 Matthew 17:1-8
10 Mark 8:34,35
11 Isaiah 30:10, 11
12 Psalm 5:5,6
13 Proverbs 3:34
14 James 4:10
15 Numbers 12:3
16 1 Corinthians 13:13
17 1 John 4:8
18 1 John 4:7
19 1 John 12, 15
20 John 3:16
21 Genesis 12:3
22 John 14:6
23 1 Timothy 2:4,-6
24 1 John 10
25 1 John 11
26 Mark 1:11
27 John 14:31
28 John 17:6
29 John 17:20
30 John 17:10
31 John 17:12
32 Isaiah 42:10, 12
33 Luke 15:20
34 Luke 15:24
35 Luke 15:10
36 1 Corinthians 13:4–8

Epilogue

1 Hebrews 10:10

ABOUT THE AUTHOR

Stephen Schey grew up in a Christian home but didn't come to a personal faith until well into adulthood. He had been blessed in working in many different secular occupations and while never serving as a pastor in a local church, he has been directly involved serving as administrator for two large churches and leading or attending Bible studies and groups. He claims no new revelations in this work but affirms the Bible as the authority and Word of God as the source of wisdom and understanding. For those who dare to truly seek answers to life's difficult questions, they can be found. Steve currently resides in Wickenburg, Arizona with his wife, Ellen and is blessed with three children, seven grandchildren and two great-grandchildren.

www.ingramcontent.com/pod-product-compliance
Lightning Source LLC
Chambersburg PA
CBHW060522130626
46553CB00002B/609